# NOT TILL THE FAT LADY SINGS

The most dramatic finishes in **Detroit** sports history

FOREWORD BY
**MICHAEL ROSENBERG**

EDITED BY
**AL TOBY**

**Detroit Free Press**

# NOT TILL THE FAT LADY SINGS

**COPYRIGHT © 2006 BY DETROIT FREE PRESS**

Library of Congress Cataloging-in-Publication Data available upon request

This book is available in quantity at special discounts for your group or organization. For further information, contact:

**TRIUMPH BOOKS**
542 South Dearborn Street
Suite 750
Chicago, Illinois 60605
(312) 939-3330
Fax (312) 663-3557

Printed in U.S.A.
**ISBN-13:** 978-1-57243-894-1
**ISBN-10:** 1-57243894-0
Design by Ryan Ford

**INSIDE COVER**
Mickey Cochrane photo by Associated Press
Isiah Thomas photo by Detroit Free Press
Gary Player photo by Detroit Free Press
Bo Schembechler photo by Associated Press
Tara Lipinski photo by Julian H. Gonzalez/DFP
Mickey Lolich photo by Detroit Free Press
Designed by Ryan Ford

# TABLE OF CONTENTS

"They were all jumping around, celebrating at half-court. ... I saw I had a chance to steal it. No question they thought they had us, but you can't blame them. It was luck, no question about it."

**LARRY BIRD,** on his steal in Game 5 of the 1987 Eastern Conference finals

"Bo told us Thursday that he wanted us to run and play our best game ever, to play like we never have before, and then he came to my room last night and said there would be some creases and holes."

JAMIE MORRIS, on his 1986 rushing performance against Ohio State

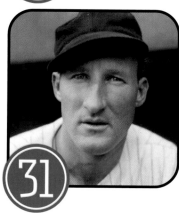

"I know I'll never forget this game. I can live without the way it turned out, but, otherwise, it was a hell of a night."

**KELLY TRIPUCKA,** on his feelings after losing, 127-123, to the Knicks in Game 5 of the first round of the 1984 NBA playoffs

# Choosing magical moments? Not as simple as you'd think

By **MICHAEL ROSENBERG**

**P**eople have the dumbest notions about what we do in the Free Press Sports department. They think we just eat cheeseburgers at the Anchor Bar and chat about sports and call it work, then have the gall to charge the cheeseburgers to our expense account. Ridiculous.

In the case of this book, we went to Nemo's.

It's good work if you can get it, but not necessarily easy work — not if you want to do it right. How do you even begin to rank the greatest finishes in Detroit sports history?

Where, for example, do you rank the Pistons' Chauncey Billups nailing a half-court shot to force overtime against New Jersey in the playoffs, which led to a second overtime ... and finally a third overtime ... which the Pistons lost, putting them on the brink of elimination before they rallied and won the 2004 championship?

Or Michigan State star Charles Rogers making an uber-athletic catch in the end zone to apparently beat Notre Dame, only to watch the Fighting Irish's Arnaz Battle one-up him with a 60-yard touchdown catch? Or

Michigan's Remy Hamilton kicking the game-winning field goal with two seconds left at Notre Dame in 1994? Or the Tigers catching the Blue Jays down the stretch for the American League East title in 1987?

These moments all have something in common. They had people jumping in their sleep that night. A die-hard fan can give a play-by-play retelling years later, including vital information such as where that fan was sitting, and with whom. Those finishes have been passed down from generation to generation like community heirlooms — or they will be.

Oh, and one other thing.

None of them made our top 50.

It's been that kind of century.

You might think we are absolute idiots for leaving some moment or another off the list, and if that's the case, I advise you to do what I do: Blame the editors. No, I'm kidding.

This is not supposed to be a definitive list. But we did have a few guidelines. We put an emphasis on game importance

— that's why Chris Webber's infamous championship-game time-out is high on the list and Maceo Baston's similar goof in the NCAA tournament's first round didn't make the cut. We're suckers for a good controversy — the 2001 Michigan and Michigan State football teams were forgettable, but the ending of their game was a conversation topic for all-time. We also considered the context of the sport — college football lends itself to more dramatic finishes than, say, baseball, so we had higher standards for college football.

We also included several absolutely devastating losses. You might take one glance at them and think, "Ya know, I could read this, but I'd rather get a prostate exam." But being a sports fan is not just about the highs. It's about the lows. And sometimes, it's about the clock winding down and knowing that you are about to experience either the highest of highs or the lowest of lows, a moment that will send you flying through the next 24 hours or send you crawling to bed like an infant, depending on what happens when this ball drops out of the air and ...

Enjoy.

Being a sports fan is not just about the highs. It's about the lows. And sometimes, it's about the clock winding down and knowing that you are about to experience either the highest of highs or the lowest of lows ...

# First team

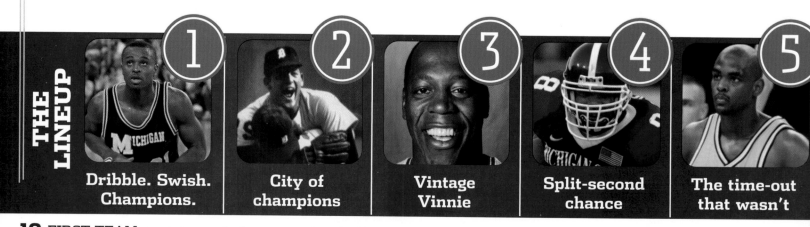

THE LINEUP

1 Dribble. Swish. Champions.

2 City of champions

3 Vintage Vinnie

4 Split-second chance

5 The time-out that wasn't

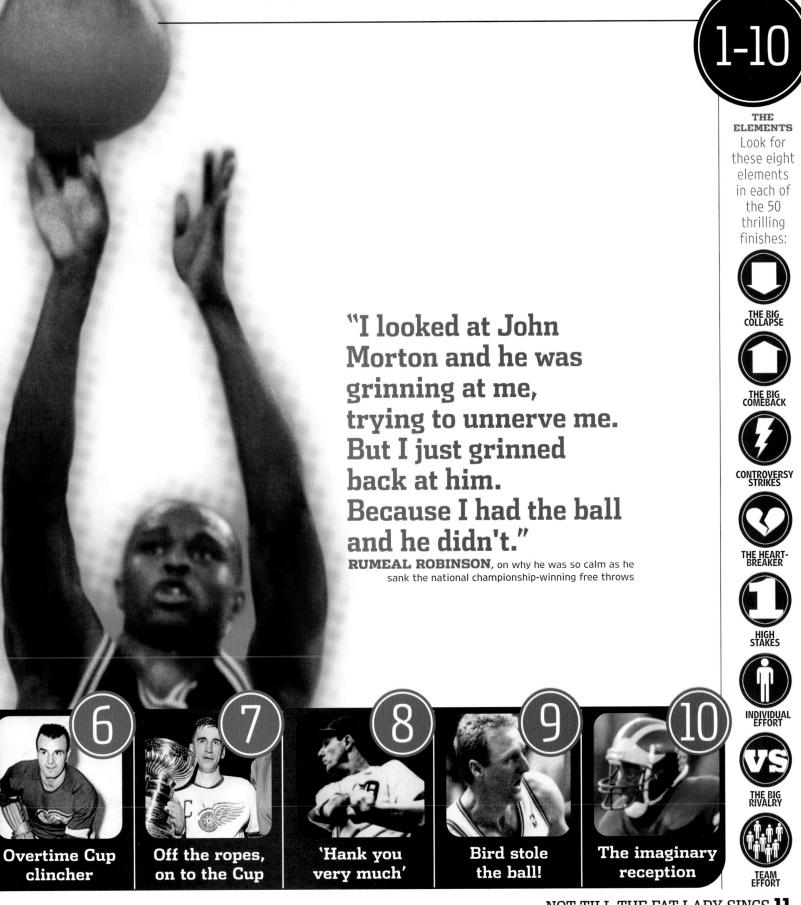

**THE ELEMENTS**
Look for these eight elements in each of the 50 thrilling finishes:

THE BIG COLLAPSE

THE BIG COMEBACK

CONTROVERSY STRIKES

THE HEART-BREAKER

HIGH STAKES

INDIVIDUAL EFFORT

THE BIG RIVALRY

TEAM EFFORT

"I looked at John Morton and he was grinning at me, trying to unnerve me. But I just grinned back at him. Because I had the ball and he didn't."
**RUMEAL ROBINSON**, on why he was so calm as he sank the national championship-winning free throws

**6** Overtime Cup clincher

**7** Off the ropes, on to the Cup

**8** 'Hank you very much'

**9** Bird stole the ball!

**10** The imaginary reception

**THE DATE:** April 3, 1989

**THE LOCATION:** The Kingdome, Seattle

**THE SETUP:**
Despite losing its coach two days before the NCAA tournament and thrusting an assistant into a high-profile role, and despite facing a late deficit and two last-second free throws, Michigan came through. It turned out to be as easy as ...

# Dribble. Shoot. Champions.

### By MITCH ALBOM

STEVEN R. NICKERSON/DETROIT FREE PRESS

**H**e stood at the free-throw line, the loneliest man in the world.

All around him was the enemy, hooting and hollering, the demons in Seton Hall uniforms talking trash, the crowd suddenly an army of "MISS IT! MISS IT!" The referee bounced the ball twice, slowly, like an executioner, and tossed it to him. Life came to a standstill. A school and a nation and a glorious destiny held their breath.

Dribble. Shoot. Swish.

Tie game.

"All right, baby!" yelled Glen Rice to Rumeal Robinson. "One more. One more."

Robinson licked his lips. What was riding on this shot? Only an entire season. Only a fairy-tale ending. Only the championship of the world in college basketball.

Pressure?

Dribble. Shoot. Swish.

Champions.

"WOOOOH! WOOOH! WOOH!" screamed Rice, hugging Robinson three seconds later, crying in his arms, after Michigan had hung on to win the NCAA championship in over-time, 80-79, in the most fantastic fin-ish to a basketball season you could ever imagine.

"WOOH! WOOH!"

Were there any other words? How else could you describe it? A game that had everything, classic theater, wonderful drama — the first over-time game in a tournament final since 1963. It had heroes and villains and magnificent plays and bonehead plays and moments when you could cut the pressure with a buzz saw, and moments when all the players, good and bad, succumbed to it.

It had Rice, named the tourna-

**"I told him God helps those who help themselves."**
**MIKE GRIFFIN**, on what he told Michigan teammate Rumeal Robinson before Robinson made his game-winning free throws

"I WAS THINKING,
'MAN, I WISH THE
REFEREE WOULD
STOP STALLING AND
GIVE ME THE BALL.'"

**RUMEAL ROBINSON**, on what he was thinking before he sank the national championship-winning free throws

ALAN R. KAMUDA/DETROIT FREE PRESS

NOT TILL THE FAT LADY SINGS **13**

STEVEN R. NICKERSON/DETROIT FREE PRESS

Hail to the Victors as they enjoy their spoils after winning the 1989 national championship against Seton Hall in overtime.

> **"They didn't know how many nights we sat up talking about a national championship. I think it was all that doubting by everyone else that enabled us to win tonight."**
>
> **SEAN HIGGINS**, on the Wolverines' motivation entering the NCAA championship game in Seattle

ment's most outstanding player, keeping his team alive all game with miracle shots, scoring from every angle, yet missing a jumper at the buzzer that could have sealed it.

It had Sean Higgins, the young, free-spirited guard sinking two clutch free throws in the final moments of regulation.

It had Steve Fisher, the interim coach, calming his team when it seemed like the world was coming down around them, when the Seton Hall Pirates were stealing everything they touched.

And finally it had Robinson, a kid who has overcome everything you can imagine, a lost childhood, academic woes, a natural shyness, to become a sterling example of what college basketball should be — and there he was, where he belonged, at the free-throw line, proving again that you can't write off any team that believes in itself.

"What were you thinking when you were standing there with the cham-

pionship on the line?" he was asked in the locker room afterward.

"I was thinking, 'Man, I wish the referee would stop stalling and give me the ball,' " he said.

Dribble. Shoot. Swish.
Champions.
Who would believe it?

"Nobody believed us," said Higgins, clutching his little brown box with the championship ring inside. "The people were all saying, 'Seton Hall, Seton Hall.' Just like at the beginning they were saying, 'Xavier, Xavier.' They didn't know how many nights we sat up talking about a national championship. I think it was all that doubting by everyone else that enabled us to win tonight."

Well, there was certainly enough of that. What a story! Who would ever believe this? A team that three weeks earlier had no coach and seemingly no chance? National champions? Not only national champions, but the first Michigan team to ever win that title. Not only national champions, but

come-from-behind national champions.

"There were moments when it got a little scary," said Rice, who scored 31 points. "Their defense was really good, and they kept getting me out of my type of offense."

The final minutes of this affair were enough to make you lose your hair, misplace your heartbeat. Michigan had squandered a 12-point lead in the second half and missed a chance to win at the regulation buzzer, when Rice's 20-footer thumped the rim once, twice and out. Overtime? Overtime.

The Wolverines fell behind, 79-76. The Seton Hall fans seemed to own the Kingdome. Each Michigan miss brought a roar and fans leaping to their feet, smelling the kill. Wasn't this supposed to be a neutral court? Where did all this blue and white come from?

But Michigan fought back. Robinson brought the ball upcourt against a chorus of jeers — "Terry, it's your shot" he yelled at Terry Mills — and Mills made that shot, a leaping banker, to cut it to 79-78. Seton Hall came back downcourt, dripping time off the clock, 20 seconds left, 10 seconds left, finally, the Pirates took a shot, it missed badly, and Rice caught the ball and dished to Robinson.

"From that point, I wanted the shot," said Robinson, who raced upcourt, drove the lane and was fouled by Gerald Greene. "I didn't want to put the burden on anyone else's shoulders."

Can you believe that? Why not? Didn't you see him at that free-throw line?

Wasn't he the picture of calm — even as your heart pounded in your throat.

"I told him, 'I made mine, now you make yours,' " Higgins said.

"I told him God helps those who help themselves," said Mike Griffin.

Everyone had a word of encouragement. Everyone had a piece of heavenly advice. But the ball was in Robinson's hands, his alone. Pressure?

"I looked at (Seton Hall's) John Morton and he was grinning at me, trying to unnerve me," Robinson said. "But I just grinned back at him. Because I had the ball and he didn't."

Dribble. Shoot. Swish. Champions.

Didn't everyone feel a little sprightlier lately?

U-M basketball did that: Rice, shooting from the heavens, breaking the NCAA tournament record for points. God, what a tournament. There are rims in Atlanta and Lexington that are still too hot to touch.

And Robinson, always with the ball, dictating the creative flow, holding in midair, then flicking in those two-footers. And Higgins, with that goofy expression and that flexible-flyer body all over the court.

DETROIT FREE PRESS

U-M's Rumeal Robinson, going one-on-one with a Pirates defender, said he wasn't giving up the ball on the Wolverines' final possession. "I didn't want to put the burden on anyone else's shoulders."

And Mills, with a wingspan like a pterodactyl, rising toward the hoop for a rebound or a jumper. And Loy Vaught, sucking in the rebounds, and Mike Griffin, the unappreciated guy — making steals or an invisible defensive maneuver. Or Mark Hughes. Or Demetrius Calip.

Look at them now, cutting down the nets. Champions.

And Steve Fisher, the interim coach. Here is the story to end all stories. The hero of second-fiddles everywhere. He replaced the departed Bill Frieder two days before the tournament and never looked back; six wins later, he became coach of the national champions.

"I am the happiest man in the world right now," Fisher said. "I couldn't be prouder of this team and what they did."

When the buzzer sounded, Robinson and Rice locked in that eternal embrace, a hug that would never end, crying, laughing, screaming, doing everything we all would do at a moment like that.

"WOOH! WOOH! WOOH!"

## INSIDE THE FINISH
# What made the end so exciting:

### A BRAND NEW COACH

Two days before the Wolverines started the 1989 NCAA tournament, athletic director Bo Schembechler named assistant Steve Fisher the interim head coach. About 26 1/2 hours before that, Michigan's original coach, Bill Frieder, was introduced as Arizona State's coach.

"Things always turn out for the best" Schembechler said. "I'm disappointed by the timing. I'm sure he will say he wanted to coach the team, but I did not want an Arizona State coach coaching Michigan. I wanted a Michigan man."

ASSOCIATED PRESS

Bill Frieder, right, took the head coaching job at Arizona State, expecting to still coach Michigan in the NCAA tournament.

### THE PERFECT SHOT

Sean Higgins hit a jumper from the left baseline with two seconds left to beat Illinois, 83-81, in the national semifinal. Higgins rebounded Terry Mills' miss. Mills got open off a screen from Glen Rice, U-M's best player in the tournament. Rice was willing to be a screener and not a shooter at the end.

Sean Higgins

"I just want to thank God for Sean Higgins," said Loy Vaught.

**THE DATE:** October 10, 1968

**THE LOCATION:** Busch Stadium, St. Louis

**THE SETUP:**
Even with an invincible Bob Gibson looming and one more loss threatening to end the World Series, the resilient Tigers had plenty of fight left. They beat Gibson, the odds and the mighty Cardinals to the punch, again making Detroit the ...

THE ELEMENTS

# City of champions

## By GEORGE CANTOR

**A**nyone looking for Detroit need not bother.

Because it isn't there.

The Tigers are champions of the world, and the whole city is seven heavens high in the air.

All the years of waiting were forgotten as the Tigers brought it all back home.

Mickey Lolich vanquished the unbeatable Bob Gibson, 4-1, in Game 7, and the Tigers completed one of the most stirring comebacks in the history of baseball.

Counted down and out a hundred different times, the Tigers fought back to beat the best the St. Louis Cardinals could throw at them.

They pounded Gibson, who had walked all over them two previous times, for a winning three-run rally in the seventh.

They took the speed game and rammed it down the Cardinals' throats, picking off their two fastest men in the same inning.

They stayed with their fledgling shortstop, and he pulled off one spectacular play after another under the greatest kind of pressure.

And at 4:06 p.m., Tim McCarver's pop foul settled into catcher Bill Freehan's big mitt along with the championship.

Freehan jumped on Lolich, who had trotted over to the first-base line on the play, then picked up his pitcher and carried him toward the dugout.

He couldn't get more than five steps though, before the rest of the Tigers descended on them in a howling, bellowing mass.

Detroit went to the strength of the Cards to beat them. The pitching wilted, the speed dried up, and a defensive play of the Cardinal strongholds decided the Series.

Curt Flood, rated the best center-fielder in baseball, misjudged a Jim Northrup liner with two runners aboard for a triple that drove in the

**"I couldn't believe it when I came around first and saw him chasing the ball behind him."**

**JIM NORTHRUP**, on Curt Flood's misplay of a triple that drove in the winning runs in Game

AND AT 4:06 P.M.,
TIM McCARVER'S
POP FOUL SETTLED
INTO BILL FREEHAN'S
BIG MITT ALONG
WITH THE
CHAMPIONSHIP.

Tigers catcher Bill Freehan hoists winning pitcher Mickey Lolich into the air after Freehan caught the final out in the 1968 World Series. Lolich started three games and won them all.

Civic pride and team spirit crept out in just about every corner of Detroit in the 1968 World Series.

DETROIT FREE PRESS

> "I knew Curt Flood played very deep, and I hoped it would drop fast enough to get in front of him. I just didn't think it was hit hard enough to get over his head."
>
> **JIM NORTHRUP**, on his winning triple past St. Louis outfielder Curt Flood

deciding runs in the seventh.

"I knew Curt Flood played very deep, and I hoped it would drop fast enough to get in front of him," Northrup said. "I just didn't think it was hit hard enough to get over his head.

"I couldn't believe it when I came around first and saw him chasing the ball behind him."

The hit broke up a scoreless duel of almost unbearable tenseness between Gibson and Lolich.

Lolich, working on two days' rest, survived a small scare in the first and then matched Gibson almost pitch-for-pitch. He finally lost his shutout with two out in the ninth when Mike Shannon socked a home run.

Gibson wound up with eight strike-outs to finish with 35, eclipsing his own record of 31 set in 1964.

Lou Brock singled in the sixth for his 13th hit of the Series. That single turned the game around.

The contest was still scoreless — Lolich pitching a two-hitter and Gibson a one-hitter — when Brock slashed one through the left side.

The big crowd came alive, screaming, "Go! Go! Go!" as the man who had thumbed his nose at the Tigers all Series started edging off first base.

Lolich's first pitch to Julian Javier was a ball. Brock moved off again — three, four, five strides from the bag — daring Lolich to do something about it.

Lolich watched him from the rubber, started his motion and instead threw to first base. Brock already had started his move to second, and first baseman Norm Cash fired to shortstop Mickey Stanley to nip him by a step.

Javier lined out, but Flood beat out a hit to deep short. He began leading off, too, and once more Lolich went to first and caught the runner taking off. Flood was hung up in a rundown, with Stanley making the tag.

And then the Tigers struck.

Gibson had mowed down 20 of the first 21 batters and looked invincible. Stanley hit a fourth-inning single to the grass behind shortstop, and other balls had been hit hard, but Gibson seemed the complete master of the situation.

The first two hitters in the seventh went down. Then Cash lined a sharp single to right. Willie Horton picked on the next pitch and grounded a single between third and short, with Cash stopping at second.

That brought up Northrup, who accounted for the Tigers' run off Gibson with a homer in the 10-1 loss in Game 4.

Northrup sent a sharp liner to straightaway center. Flood came in on the ball and seemed to have a bead on it.

Suddenly, he stopped and frantically tried to pivot and head back on the drive. His spikes slipped on the turf, still damp from rain a day earlier, and he almost fell to his knees.

The ball sailed far over his head as Northrup raced to third with a triple.

Freehan, with one hit in 22 at-bats, came up next. He had hit the ball right on the button his first two times up, but both were caught. This time he drilled a sinking liner to left-field. Brock missed a shoestring catch, and the ball fell in safely for a double, scoring Northrup.

That made it 3-0, but the Tigers had one parting shot left for Gibson. The right-hander was permitted to hit for himself in the eighth as St. Louis hoped he could check the Tigers without a run in the ninth to keep them within striking distance. But he couldn't.

Horton and Northrup ripped consecutive one-out singles. Freehan fouled out, but Don Wert, 1-for-16 in the Series, laced a single to center to bring in the final run. Both of Wert's

hits came off Gibson.

Lolich, backed by outstanding defense, pitched over everything. A single by Flood and a walk to Orlando Cepeda put two on in the first, but Shannon's fly to right was caught by Al Kaline.

Stanley made a beautiful short-hop pickup on a smash by Roger Maris in the second to start a double play.

Stanley and Wert turned in back-to-back gems in the fourth to knock down bullets by Flood and Cepeda.

Even a two-base error in the seventh — when Northrup and Horton ran together on a short fly ball — couldn't faze the unflappable Lolich. He calmly got the next two batters to end the inning.

When he walked Brock on four pitches with two gone in the eighth, manager Mayo Smith made his only appearance on the field. But on the next play, Wert raced in to one-hop a bunt by Javier and throw him out.

Flood led off the ninth with a liner that Ray Oyler, who had just gone in at shortstop, speared going to his right.

Cepeda fouled to Freehan to the left of the plate.

Shannon then drilled one out of the park for the first run off Lolich in 16 innings. It was only the second run the Cards had scored since the first inning of Game 5.

McCarver then hoisted a towering foul that Freehan caught along the first-base line to end the Series.

Lolich became the second left-hander to win three games in a Series.

Lolich also won the sports car presented annually by Sport Magazine to the outstanding player in the Series.

Maybe he can trade it in for a 400-horsepower motorcycle.

## INSIDE THE FINISH
# What made the end so exciting:

**GAME 5: THE PLAY THAT CHANGED THE SERIES**

TONY SPINA/DETROIT FREE PRESS

Catcher Bill Freehan stops St. Louis outfielder Lou Brock in the crucial play of Game 5 of the 1968 World Series. The Tigers were trailing in the Series, 3-1.

The Roadrunner's beep-beeps were turned into bloop-bloops by the Tigers in Game 5 of the World Series. But Lou Brock wasn't happy about it.

The brilliant Cardinals out-fielder pointed to the fifth-inning call on him at home plate as the one that meant the difference between victory and defeat for the Cards.

"He called me out for not touching the plate," Brock said. "But I don't feel that I touched it, I KNOW I did.

"I beat the ball to the plate — that's why I didn't slide. I know I was safe."

Brock cited the play on which Tigers leftfielder Willie Horton's throw to Bill Freehan after Julian Javier's single got him at home.

It deprived St. Louis of a 4-2 lead and perhaps further rallying in the fifth.

"As it turned out it was the biggest play of the game — the turning point," he said, softly but firmly. "He (umpire Doug Harvey) called it immediately, and there hadn't been a tag."

"While I was arguing, Freehan came up behind me and tagged me — he knew I had touched the plate.

"The instant replay showed I touched it," Brock added a bit more heatedly. "WE all saw it when they flashed it on the TV monitor by the dugout." Trailing by one run in the seventh, the Tigers pulled it out in the late innings.
By Jack Saylor

**THE DATE:** June 14, 1990

**THE LOCATION:** Memorial Coliseum, Portland, Ore.

**THE SETUP:**
Needing one basket for a second straight NBA championship, the Pistons had plenty of options – captain Isiah, Joe D. or Laimbeer – but when it came to crunch time against the Blazers, Chuck Daly's squad called on and got ...

THE ELEMENTS

WILLIAM ARCHIE/DETROIT FREE PRESS

# Vintage Vinnie

BY CORKY MEINECKE

**P**istons captain Isiah Thomas called it "vintage Vinnie."

How else would one describe the jumper that guard Vinnie Johnson nailed, the one with :00.7 second left that beat the Portland Trail Blazers, 92-90, and gave the Pistons their second straight NBA title?

It came in the clutch, with 6-foot-7 Trail Blazers forward Jerome Kersey directly in his face.

"I never made a shot like that before," Johnson said afterward as champagne dripped off his baseball cap. "I used to do it all the time in college, but this was the first time I did it in the pros."

That's news to the Pistons.

"It was a great shot, but a typical Vinnie Johnson shot," said center Bill Laimbeer. "I've seen him make that kind of shot a thousand times. He is a playground player, a Brooklyn player, and that's the kind of shot he's always been able to make at any level he's played."

Guard Joe Dumars agreed.

"Vinnie makes so many shots like that," he said. "If anybody else had taken a shot so off-balance, I might have worried. But not with Vinnie."

Johnson certainly couldn't have picked a better time, what with overtime looming. The 14-foot shot was

> **"I've seen him make that kind of shot a thousand times. He is a playground player, a Brooklyn player, and that's the kind of shot he's always been able to make at any level he's played."**
> **BILL LAIMBEER**, on guard Vinnie Johnson, left, after Johnson made a jumper to give the Pistons their second straight NBA title

Vinnie Johnson's winning jumper touched off a wet and wild victory celebration in the Pistons' locker room.

"I dream about this all the time, but I'm not usually in the game, so I don't get the opportunity. I guess you could say it's a dream come true."

**VINNIE JOHNSON,** on his title-winning shot with 0.7 seconds remaining

DETROIT FREE PRESS

James (Buddha) Edwards averaged 14.3 points and 3.6 rebounds for the Pistons in the 1990 playoffs.

the punctuation mark on another stirring comeback by the Pistons, who were down by seven points with two minutes left.

"Only an incredible one-on-one player could do that," said coach Chuck Daly. "Now you know why we protected him last year from the expansion draft. I know a lot of you guys questioned it at the time, but he

proved it was the right move tonight."

After last year's Finals, many thought the Pistons would leave Johnson unprotected. He wasn't pro-

DETROIT FREE PRESS

Coach Chuck Daly protected Vinnie Johnson from an expansion draft — a move that paid off big-time.

tected in the 1988 expansion draft, but neither the Charlotte Hornets nor Miami Heat took him. To the surprise of everyone, the Pistons left Rick Mahorn unprotected last season, and the Minnesota Timberwolves pounced on him.

Not all of Game 5 went well for Johnson, who slumped earlier in the playoffs. He struggled in the first half — 0-for-3 shooting, three fouls, one turnover — but he was bothered by a sore knee. The knee limbered up in the second half, much to the Trail Blazers' chagrin. Johnson finished with 16 points on 6-for-11 shooting.

And he saved the best for last.

"On Detroit's winning shot, we had the play defensed," said Portland coach Rick Adelman. "Jerome had his hand in Vinnie's face. It's such a great advantage for Detroit to be able to bring such a good third guard off the bench."

Johnson credited Laimbeer.

"I was kind of down on myself in the first half, and Bill kept me in the game," he said. "I dream about this all the time, but I'm not usually in the game, so I don't get the opportunity. I guess you could say it's a dream come true."

## INSIDE THE FINISH
# What made the end so exciting:

### JUST CLOSE ENOUGH

**1** The series was lopsided, but the games weren't one-sided. A case could be made that the 1990 NBA Finals between the Pistons and Portland Trail Blazers was the most exciting championship round decided in five games.

Four games had a combined winning differential of 12 points. One game went overtime and three weren't decided until the final shot.

In Game 1, Isiah Thomas set the tone for the series in the fourth quarter, scoring 16 of his 33 points to spark a comeback.

The Pistons trailed, 90-80, with 7:05 left. Thomas did all his scoring after that point — including 10 in a 2:26 stretch.

In Game 2, it appeared Bill Laimbeer's incredible 25-foot three-pointer would make the Pistons 105-104 winners with 4.1 seconds left in overtime. But on the Blazers' next possession, Clyde Drexler was fouled by Dennis Rodman as he drove from the free-throw line. Drexler sank two free throws with 2.1 seconds left. Portland's Cliff Robinson blocked James Edwards' midrange jump shot the instant before time expired.

In Game 4, the Pistons led, 110-109, with 6.5 seconds left. The Pistons took the ball out of bounds. They beat Portland's press as Edwards hit Gerald Henderson alone near the bas-

DETROIT FREE PRESS

Bill Laimbeer soaks up the festivities after the Pistons won their second straight title. Laimbeer narrowly missed being the hero of Game 2, Detroit's only loss in the series.

ket. Rather than dribbling the clock dry, Henderson took a lay-up, and Portland got the ball with 1.8 seconds left.

Danny Young sank a long three-pointer — but it was after the clock expired.

**By Steve Kornacki and Drew Sharp**

**THE DATE:** November 3, 2001

**THE LOCATION:** Spartan Stadium, East Lansing

**THE SETUP:**
Just when it looked like time had run out on the host Spartans in another heartbreaking loss to the Wolverines, time stood still – or so it seemed to U-M fans. MSU's Jeff Smoker and T.J. Duckett took advantage of their ...

**THE ELEMENTS**

# Split-second chance

ERIC SEALS/DETROIT FREE PRESS

T.J. Duckett rushed for 211 yards against Michigan, but it was his touchdown catch with no time left that gave the Spartans the win.

BY JEMELE HILL

**J**eff Smoker was on his knees crying. T.J. Duckett was sprawled out in the end zone with what seemed like several hundred people smothering him. Michigan linebacker Larry Foote was hunting down game officials to give them a piece of his mind.

The scene that unfolded after Michigan State's 26-24 upset victory over sixth-ranked Michigan capped one of the most bizarre, thrilling and controversial games of this rivalry.

With no time left, MSU junior tailback T.J. Duckett hauled in the game-winning touchdown that gave the Wolverines their first loss in the Big Ten season and ruined any hopes they might have had for a national title.

But depending on whether you're a Spartan or a Wolverine, either a very good team was beaten or a very good team was cheated.

The winning play itself was not controversial. On a play named "Slant F-crash," quarterback Smoker rolled right and lofted a pass over cornerback Marlin Jackson that landed right in Duckett's midsection.

The controversy occurred two plays before Duckett's winning catch. The Spartans were second-and-goal on the 3 with 17 seconds left. Smoker rolled right and looked for an open receiver, and when there wasn't one, he tried to run it in himself.

Smoker was tackled after a one-yard gain with 12 seconds left, and the Spartans had no time-outs left. By the time he got up, gathered his teammates to the line of scrimmage and stopped the clock by spiking the ball, there was one second remaining.

Or was there?

The Spartans say the clock operated just fine. And though most of the

"Our players deserve better."

**LLOYD CARR**, Michigan coach, on the officiating, particularly the timekeeping in the game's final seconds

Michigan State's Monquiz Wedlow shares the joy with Spartan fans after MSU's last-second upset of Michigan in 2001.

Wolverines didn't say much, Foote spoke for the whole team when he angrily sought out the officials after the game.

"Hey, I don't run the clock," said MSU coach Bobby Williams, shrugging his shoulders.

Said Smoker: "It was close, but we had the ball spiked in time."

Said Michigan coach Lloyd Carr: "Our players deserve better," referring to the officiating.

Besides, the Wolverines should reserve some blame for themselves. Michigan committed two key penalties during that last drive, helping ignite the Spartans' comeback.

On fourth-and-16 at midfield, Smoker threw an incomplete pass to wide receiver Herb Haygood. The game should have been over, but sophomore Jeremy LeSueur grabbed the face mask of wide receiver Charles Rogers. Michigan was assessed a 15-yard penalty, and the Spartans had a first down.

"He just locked onto it and drug me out of bounds," said Rogers, who drew three pass-interference calls and had six catches for 86 yards, including a 17-yard touchdown in the first quarter.

Three plays later, the Spartans were first-and-10 on the Michigan 18. Defensive tackle Grant Bowman sacked Smoker for what would have been a significant loss on two accounts because the Spartans had no time-outs. The problem? Michigan had 12 players on the field, and the penalty pushed the Spartans to the 3.

"It was huge," Williams said. "It gave us the field position we needed. That was a tough game to officiate with the emotion on the field, the talking and the extracurricular stuff that goes on. I thought they did a fantastic job."

Michigan helped, but the Spartans made the plays when

MANDI WRIGHT/DETROIT FREE PRESS

Charles Rogers, catching a touchdown against Michigan's Marlin Jackson, finished with six catches for 86 yards. He also drew three pass-interference calls and one key illegal-hands-to-the-face call late in the game.

The Spartans' end zone was party central after MSU defeated Michigan, 26-24.

ERIC SEALS/DETROIT FREE PRESS

they needed to. The Spartans faced three fourth-down situations during that drive. LeSueur's penalty bailed them out, but the other two were converted by Smoker and Duckett.

On fourth-and-three from the 11, Smoker connected with Duckett on a slant route for an eight-yard gain. And then there was the last play of the game, which came on fourth-and-goal from Michigan's 2.

The Wolverines can complain about how it ended, but the evidence shows the Spartans outplayed them.

The Wolverines' front seven sacked Smoker 12 times, but the defense gave up 211 yards to Duckett on the ground. Duckett averaged 7.8 yards per carry on the nation's No. 1 rush defense, and his total yards were the most any Spartan running back has ever gained on the Wolverines.

The Spartans' defense, which gave up 17 points in the first half, held the Wolverines to one score in the second. And the Spartans did it without one of their best defensive players, tackle Josh Shaw, who suffered a season-ending knee injury with 2:18 left in the first quarter.

Michigan wideout Marquise Walker finished with nine catches for 150 yards and two scores, but his production was slowed in the second half. He caught only four balls for 19 yards and never reached the end zone after halftime.

The secondary, supposedly MSU's weakest link after losing three starting cornerbacks in the past month to injury, picked off two John Navarre passes in the second half.

"What a win," Williams said. "This was a huge win for this program."

## INSIDE THE FINISH

# What made the end so exciting:

### THE SPARTANS' UNLIKELY HERO

Bob Stehlin knew immediately he was part of Michigan State-Michigan football lore.

He knew when MSU trustees in an adjacent Spartan Stadium skybox began shooting him thumbs-up signs. He knew when university employees popped their heads into his booth to thank him.

They were ecstatic that the man known to many as Spartan Bob had stopped the clock with one second left at the end of MSU's biggest game of 2001.

One second that the game's broadcasters, Michigan coaches and at least half the state didn't think should be there.

One second that his beloved Spartans used to win the game on the last play.

As the celebration began, Stehlin sat dazed, tucked in the booth, where he had worked in anonymity for 21 years.

He waited — for the trustees to file out, for the reporters down the hall in the press box to leave, for the whole stadium to grow quiet and dark so he could slink into the night.

Stehlin, who avoided media, broke his silence in 2003, after retiring as a timekeeper for MSU football, basketball, volleyball and field hockey. Frank Beckmann, Michigan's play-by-play radio announcer, called the incident criminal. Stehlin blames Beckmann for the odd celebrity he achieved afterward.

In East Lansing, and in homes of Spartans fans around the state, Stehlin is the man who helped beat Michigan. In Ann Arbor, he's known as the homer who stole the game.

No one, save the people he worked for in the athletic department and a handful of friends, knew who he was.

RASHAUN RUCKER/DETROIT FREE PRESS

Scoreboard operator Bob Stehlin kept a low profile after the controversial game in 2001. That didn't stop at least one U-M fan from finding him.

About a month after the Michigan game, Stehlin got word from the athletic department that someone had filed Freedom of Information Act paperwork with the university to access his employee records. It scared him.

Not long after that, a card arrived in his home mail. It was a thank-you note, dripping with maize-and-blue sarcasm. The writer had learned through his personnel files that he was Catholic and had served in the military.

The card suggested he confess his game-clock sin. To further cleanse his green-and-white soul, he was told to come clean to his former commanding officer.

"A lawyer sent it," Stehlin said. "He was from southeast Michigan."

All along, Stehlin felt he did the right thing. "My job," he said. "If it had been Michigan in that situation, they would've had the second."

The Monday after the game, back at work, his boss told him he thought his finger was a little quick. But later in the week, he got his first reassurance when Big Ten officials reviewed the game and said they found nothing wrong.

Stehlin wanted a public acknowledgement from the Big Ten or even from MSU that he had done his job, mostly to placate Ann Arbor. He never got it.

"They had their reasons, I guess," he said.

**By Shawn Windsor**

**THE DATE:** April 5, 1993

**THE LOCATION:** Superdome, New Orleans

**THE SETUP:**
Time was winding down in the NCAA title game. The never-give-up Wolverines trailed the Tar Heels by two points. In what proved to be the Fab Five's last act, Chris Webber grabbed a late rebound, charged down the court and called for ...

**THE ELEMENTS**

# The time-out that wasn't

By MITCH ALBOM

It ended with Chris Webber looking desperately for something he didn't have — time, hope, help. With his team trailing by two points, he grabbed a rebound and called for time. He screamed for it. The ref stared at him blankly.

Confused, Webber muscled his way up the court, panic in his eyes. He traveled, but this one man-against-everything journey seemed to have everyone's tongue tied, including the referee's. And so here was Webber, clock ticking down, still running, still dribbling, pounding the ball with his giant hands, going past his bench, wanting help, wanting a time-out, no one able to make clear to him that, Chris, we don't have any time-outs left.

Finally, he pulled up, stopped, like a man who realizes he is cornered by police. He made the "T" sign, looked at the ref, who made the "T" sign right back.

Technical foul.

Disaster.

"We were screaming, 'No time-outs! No time-outs!' " James Voskuil said in the dejected locker room after Michigan lost the NCAA championship game to North Carolina, 77-71. "But with all that noise and all those people screaming, 'No time-out,' who knows? Maybe all you hear is 'Time-out!' And he called for one."

And with that, the run on destiny that these Wolverines had made, against amazing odds, all the way to the end of the college basketball rainbow, was over.

And instead of a U-M celebration,

Wolverines cutting down nets, the sad final picture of the 1993 season would be this: The Fab Five standing on the half-court line, watching helplessly as North Carolina sank the two technical free throws that put this game out of reach.

Ray Jackson was on one knee, as if praying. Juwan Howard looked like he had lost a friend. Jimmy King had his hands on his hips. Jalen Rose had his head lowered. And Webber, well, he was stunned. All he had done, all the slams, the monster rebounds, the steals, the baskets he made falling, his 23 points, his 11 boards, his 33 minutes — all that, gone in a simple, desperate mistake.

"I cost us the game," he mumbled afterward. "I cost us the game."

He left the postgame podium and shut himself inside a staff room, and

"But with all that noise and all those people screaming, 'No time-out,' who knows? Maybe all you hear is 'Time-out!' And he called for one."
**JAMES VOSKUIL**, on Chris Webber's infamous time-out that cost the Wolverines a shot at winning the national championship

"I COST US THE GAME. I COST US THE GAME."

**CHRIS WEBBER**, on attempting to call a time-out in the closing seconds of the NCAA championship game

SUSAN RAGAN/ASSOCIATED PRESS

"It's hard. I don't know what you do ... except try to hug him."

**STEVE FISHER,** on how you console a player who makes a mental mistake in the NCAA championship game like Chris Webber did

DETROIT FREE PRESS

The Fab Five: Jalen Rose, foreground, and from left, Juwan Howard, Jimmy King, Ray Jackson and Chris Webber were the rock stars of college hoops.

he didn't emerge for almost an hour. He walked quickly toward the bus, eyes forward, fighting everything inside him, ignoring reporters, ignoring the lights, ignoring everything until one of his younger brothers came up and hugged him, and Chris Webber could hold it no more. He began to cry. His father stepped up and hugged him, too, and now Chris began to sob. He was, at that moment, in the hallway of a stadium 1,000 miles from home, what we always forget that each of these college basketball players is:

A kid.

"I cost us the game."

In the sadness of that moment, you almost don't want to analyze it. A basketball game is 40 minutes long, and every bad play counts the same.

You only remember the last ones.

But OK. The truth is, they'll be talking about it forever, so for what it's worth, here is the responsibility chain: The coach is supposed to make sure the players know the time-out situation. The coach is supposed to get the players' eyes when he is in doubt. According to most of the players, Steve Fisher did tell his players they were out of time-outs in their last huddle.

"But whether everyone heard it," said Rose, "well, you know, there's a lot goin' on."

Said Fisher, "We thought we said it, but apparently we didn't get specific enough."

Later, Fisher was near tears in his sorrow and his sympathy for Webber.

"It's hard," he whispered, when

asked how he could make a player feel better after that. "I don't know what you do ... except try to hug him."

Yes. And tell him that without his courage, his excellence, getting off the floor with a bad eye poke and coming back to score a basket, stealing the ball and dribbling the length of the floor for a slam, without that, this wasn't even a close game. In fact Michigan seemed all but finished before Webber came down with that rebound.

"When he got it, I said to myself: 'It's Michigan's ballgame.'" Rose said later. "But you know, the whole night was unusual. It was like I looked up and there were two minutes left and I was like, where did the game go?"

Indeed, the whole game took less

than two hours to play, including all the TV interruptions. The first half was a tug of war, Michigan opening tightly, then exploding for a 10-point lead, then falling back to a six-point halftime deficit.

And the second half? It was quick and seemed like forever. At times it was so brutal, so intense, force on force, defense vs. defense, that it felt like someone trying to push a refrigerator up the stairs. Minutes would pass without a good shot. The defenses were like soggy blankets. It was less a game than a slugfest, one in which the referee just lets them go at each other, to the body, to the head, the body, the head, last one standing wins. "It was," Fisher said afterward, "what I expected. A game that went down to the wire."

But the ending he didn't expect. So many times Michigan had pulled off this type of miracle. The Wolverines don't lose overtime games in the postseason. They don't lose in crunch time. Isn't that their reputation?

And when Pat Sullivan missed the second free throw with 19 seconds left, the Wolverines were perched on another great finish. How terribly sad then, that the game slipped out of Webber's hands, even as he cradled the ball.

What is important is a salute to effort. The Wolverines didn't lose this game because of trash-talking or a bad attitude. They turned the ball over too often and had a few disastrous plays at the end. King shooting an air ball. Rose losing a pass inside that was stolen. Any of those things happen in the final seconds, and we're feeling sorry for another Wolverine instead of Webber.

## INSIDE THE FINISH

# What made the end so exciting:

### THE HEART-STOPPER BEFORE THE HEARTBREAKER

TUCSON, Ariz. — Fab (Forty) Five.

Minutes. Not players. You know the word. The word doesn't fit. It's not enough. Not for either team. Not for this game.

To call Michigan's pulsating, 86-84 overtime conquest of UCLA something as mild as fabulous is to damn it with the faintest of praise. The top-seeded Wolverines and ninth-seeded Bruins rocked McKale Center for 45 excruciating minutes in an NCAA tournament West Regional second-round game.

"We're on cloud nine," Michigan coach Steve Fisher said. "They're on death row."

UCLA owned the first half. Michigan owned the second. Bizarre owned the overtime.

Michigan, rooted in sophomores, triumphed because one of them — Jimmy King — scored on a rebound with less than two seconds left in OT. Then there was confusion.

The Wolverines had set up the final play during a time-out with 9.6 seconds left on the game clock and seven seconds on the 45-second shot clock. Jalen Rose drove off a left-side pick, pulled up for a jumper and banked it off the backboard. He took the shot with one second on the shot clock.

JULIAN H. GONZALEZ/DETROIT FREE PRESS

Jimmy King was the hero in the second round of the 1993 NCAA tournament for Michigan, scoring the game-winning basket in U-M's overtime win against UCLA.

The ball bounced off the glass and caught the front of the rim before King grabbed the rebound on the right side.

The shot-clock buzzer sounded just after Rose released his shot. Because he did beat that buzzer with the release — and the shot subsequently hit the rim — it was a legal attempt and no violation.

**By Greg Stoda**

**THE DATE:** April 23, 1950

**THE LOCATION:** Olympia Stadium, Detroit

**THE SETUP:**
For the first time ever, Game 7 of the Stanley Cup finals went into overtime. Then it went into a second overtime. Finally, Red Wing Pete Babando scored his second goal of the game for the ...

# Overtime Cup clincher

By **MARSHALL DANN**

The Stanley Cup returned to Detroit for the first time since 1943.

On a dramatic overtime goal by Pete Babando, a "poor cousin" on the Detroit squad most of the season, the Wings scored a 4-3 victory in the seventh and deciding game of the finals against the New York Rangers.

The path to the Cup was rocky, and the last mile was the roughest. The Wings fought an uphill battle for the second straight night to pull a game out of the fire.

Trailing, 2-0, in the first period, they erupted for three goals in the second period to tie it, 3-all. Then the teams played scoreless hockey for more than 52 minutes before Babando came through.

The end came at 12:14 a.m. with Babando slapping home a backhand shot from 15 feet after 28:31 of overtime play.

It was the second goal of the game for Babando, who was shunted to the role of benchwarmer for most of the series.

Detroit's other tallies were from Sid Abel and Jimmy McFadden. Al Stanley, Tony Leswick and Buddy O'Connor paraded goalward in that order for New York.

The game would have ended much sooner but for the stubbornness of Ranger goalie Chuck Rayner. He made 40 saves, 15 in overtime. Harry Lumley stopped 26 at the other end.

It marked the first time in Cup history that a seventh and deciding game went into overtime. But then, these playoffs have been wacky all along.

Detroit went the full seven games in the semifinal against Toronto, winning the sixth and seventh games to survive.

Then the Wings had more trouble with the Rangers, whose fight and play belied their fourth-place standing. Detroit had to win Game 6, 5-4, to force the seventh game.

It was the fourth time Detroit had won the Stanley Cup, but it was the first time it had done it on home ice.

Clarence Campbell, president of the NHL, handed the big silver mug to Captain Abel in center-ice ceremonies, while the 13,095 fans at Olympia still were cheering Babando for his climactic goal.

Abel, defenseman Jack Stewart and forward Joe Carveth are the only members of the squad who dated back to the 1943 triumph.

From the time the overtime action

**From the time the overtime action started, it was Detroit's game, but it took a long time to prove it. The Wings carried play throughout the first extra 20 minutes but were wild with their shots.**

DETROIT FREE PRESS

Pete Babando scored two goals in the playoffs in 1950. Both goals came in Game 7 of the Stanley Cup finals, including his double-overtime winner.

started, it was Detroit's game, but it took a long time to prove it. The Wings carried play throughout the first extra 20 minutes but were wild with their shots.

They had chances galore in the second overtime, but the goal just wouldn't come. George Gee almost ended it seconds before he fed Babando the pass for the clincher. Finally, Rayner yielded under the terrific pressure.

For a while during the regulation 60 minutes, it looked as if the Red Wings were going to follow the same script used in Game 6.

Again the Rangers got off to an early two-goal lead. And again the Wings fought from behind twice to tie the score at 2-all and 3-all.

New York grabbed its 2-0 edge in the first 13 minutes, and Detroit didn't enter the scoring until the five-minute mark of the second period. Then the Wings added two more within 10 minutes.

Fisticuffs broke out for the first time in the series midway in the first stanza, when Ted Lindsay took a swing at Ed LaPrade in a pileup at the net.

Both swung sticks, and Lindsay drew two minors, LaPrade one.

While Lindsay was in the penalty box, the Rangers grabbed both their early tallies. LaPrade was back when Stanley drove in for the opener. He dove while speeding toward the net and just managed to deflect Leswick's pass home.

Marty Pavelich joined Lindsay with his second penalty, and the Wings were two men short for 51 seconds. The Rangers scored then, Leswick racing down the boards to rap in LaPrade's pass.

The Wings hadn't made a threat of note, and it looked

dark until a sudden spurt after Stanley's penalty four minutes after the second period opened.

Bang, bang went two Detroit goals, and the score was tied within 20 seconds on the power play.

Babando delivered his first goal of the playoffs at 5:09 with an easy kill of Red Kelly's pass out.

Then Abel slipped in from the side and fired a seven-footer through Rayner's legs at 5:30.

The tie didn't last long. New York moved in front again, 3-2, when O'Connor knocked in a short shot past Lumley from a scramble at the net.

Four minutes later it was tied again on a lucky break.

McFadden raced over the goal line, chasing Jimmy Peters' wide shot, and centered the puck back. It hit Rayner's skates while he was standing alongside the net and caromed into the goal.

After a barrage of goals like that, the 3-3 score didn't seem likely to hold for long, but it stood up through the third period and into the overtime.

With the Cup riding on every shot, Detroit carried a heavy edge in the first extra 20 minutes. The Wings outshot New York, 10-4, but Rayner was equal to every test.

McFadden, Gerry Couture and Babando missed open corners of the net with hurried shots from close range.

Rayner's best saves were against Kelly and McFadden, and Pavelich came closest to ending the game on his play off McFadden's rebound.

Pavelich speared the loose puck and lifted it toward the goal, but it hit the post precisely and bounced away harmlessly.

**THE DATE:** April 16, 1954

**THE LOCATION:** Olympia Stadium, Detroit

**THE SETUP:**
Montreal had won two straight games to force Game 7 of the Stanley Cup finals. In the finale, goalie Terry Sawchuk held off the defending champs and Tony Leswick took the Wings ...

# Off the ropes and on to the Cup

### By MARSHALL DANN and BOB LATSHAW

Tony Leswick was carried off the ice at Olympia by Detroit hockey fans and his teammates — the greatest tribute ever paid a Red Wing player as a result of one of the greatest Red Wing victories.

Leswick's goal in sudden-death overtime brought the Stanley Cup back to Detroit for the sixth time.

It ended the seventh decisive game of the finals against Montreal's defending champions in Detroit's favor, 2-1.

The Wings were on the ropes, and the record hockey crowd of 15,791 knew it when Leswick fired the decisive shot after 4:29 of overtime.

It was a routine effort when it started. Leswick's drive from near the right boards had neither speed nor sting.

Gerry McNeil, the terrific little

Montreal goalie, knew a shot was on its way, but he couldn't tell exactly where it was headed. Metro Prystai and Montreal defenseman Doug Harvey blocked his view.

That shot suddenly became the biggest goal of the entire 1953-54 season. It slipped cleanly over McNeil's upraised right arm and high into the Montreal cage.

In the Montreal dressing room, Harvey said he made a grab for the puck Leswick fired, and "it ticked off my glove into the net."

Pandemonium broke loose when the red light flashed after Leswick's goal. Teammates pummeled him in joy. Goaltender Terry Sawchuk was wrestled to the ice by his fellow Wings as he waddled from the far end of the arena.

Every time Leswick appeared out of the jumbled mass of players, the 15,971 customers rattled the rafters

with a cheer.

Ted Lindsay, the captain, accepted the trophy along with Marguerite and Bruce Norris, the co-owners, and general manager Jack Adams. NHL president Clarence Campbell made the presentation.

Some might claim that Detroit got a fluke victory on a screened shot.

But that was the way Montreal scored its lone goal to take the lead midway in the first. Floyd Curry directed it from 50 feet out, and Sawchuk was screened all the way.

Red Kelly got the equalizer early in the second stanza on a clean power-play drive. Alex Delvecchio and Lindsay handled the relays that set up Kelly 15 feet off the left side.

But the scoring plays didn't cover all the stars of the game. Sawchuk stands foremost among the others.

Going against an inspired club that had the advantage in stamina and

> ## "It ticked off my glove into the net."
> **DOUG HARVEY**, Montreal defenseman, on how Tony Leswick's shot went into the net in Game 7 of the 1954 Stanley Cup finals

DETROIT FREE PRESS

From left, Wings president Marguerite Norris, general manager Jack Adams, captain Ted Lindsay and owner Bruce Norris bask in the glory of the Stanley Cup after the 1954 finals.

manpower, the Wings gambled. They risked all on building an early lead and outfired Montreal, 25-10, in the first two periods.

That was only good enough to break even, however, and the Canadiens, using four forward lines without letup against Detroit's three, gradually took control of the game.

Unless the Wings could come up with a winning goal early in the overtime, it appeared certain that Montreal would win. Sawchuk couldn't keep making his magnificent saves forever.

Detroit's two other forward combinations got the first crack in overtime.

The Prystai-Bill Dineen-Johnny Wilson line got in 45 seconds of effort without a shot. Then the big line of Delvecchio-Gordie Howe-Lindsay tried for two and a half

minutes, with no better luck.

On came Leswick's line, with Glen Skov and Marty Pavelich. They too, could do little more than tie up the Canadiens.

Skov's forechecking suddenly proved fatal to Montreal. He slapped at Elmer Lach's attempted pass, and Leswick outfought Rocket Richard for the puck. Leswick fired, and it was over.

Leswick, a 5-foot-6 scrapper noted throughout hockey as a defensive specialist, had tallied only six goals all season.

From the opening minute, it was one of the greatest games ever played on the local ice.

Instead of the defensive tactics expected in such a crucial game, both sides gave a dramatic display of the fierce hockey for which they are noted.

McNeil had his hottest work

in the early stages, particularly against Marcel Pronovost. Sawchuk had all his tough ones in the third period. Each had only one soft save in overtime.

The break of the game almost came with a few seconds left in regulation time.

Gilles Dube, a former Montreal player the Wings called up from Sherbrooke, took a desperation 90-foot lob shot just before the siren.

The puck landed 15 feet out from the net and took a crazy hop past McNeil, who had glided out for an attempted block. The puck missed the empty net by less than six inches.

That would have been a cruel way to win the Stanley Cup. But the Wings would have been glad to apologize at that stage.

No excuses were needed for the triumph, however. The Canadiens were bidding for a

big upset, having trailed by a 3-1 margin at one stage in the series. Montreal not only had won the last two games but also had defeated Detroit in the last pair at Olympia.

The charm simply wore off both the team and McNeil, who didn't allow the Wings to shoot a single puck past him in the two previous games.

One was a 1-0 overtime shutout, the other a 4-1 victory in which his own teammates pushed the puck in for Detroit.

All that forced the Wings into a final-game effort to save their honor. By proving that they still were the best "big game" team in hockey, able to come through in the clutch, they were spared the ignominy of blowing the Stanley Cup when far ahead as well as being a league champion that lost to a second-place outfit.

**THE DATE:** September 30, 1945

**THE LOCATION:** Sportsman's Park, St. Louis

**THE SETUP:**
On the last day of the 1945 season, the Tigers needed a win to capture the pennant and avoid a one-game playoff with Washington. The Tigers trailed, 3-2, in the ninth, with Hank Greenberg at the plate. Later, Detroit would say …

THE
ELEMENTS

# 'Hank you very much'

### By LYALL SMITH

**C**all Hank Greenberg a champion of champions!

Call him the hero of Bengaltown! Call him the man who came through with a ninth-inning home run with the bases loaded to bring the Tigers their seventh American League pennant.

Call him the man who made Steve O'Neill a flag winner for the first time in a managerial career that stretches back to 1929.

Call him all the flowery things you want, for the big leftfielder stepped up to the plate and beat the defending league champions, the St. Louis Browns, 6-3, with a home run for history.

Drama … thrills … nerve-racking realization of a frustrated team of

DETROIT FREE PRESS

Hank Greenberg gives teammate Hal Newhouser a smooch. But on the last day of the 1945 regular season, Greenberg was the one deserving of affection from his teammates.

---

"What kind of a pitch was it? I really don't know. I think it was a high one. My big scare was that it might go foul."

**HANK GREENBERG**, on the pitch he hit for a grand slam that gave the Tigers the 1945 American League pennant

One of the biggest homers Hank Greenberg hit in his Hall of Fame career happened on the last day of the 1945 regular season against the St. Louis Browns. His ninth-inning grand slam won the pennant for the Tigers. Detroit would take the World Series in seven games from the Chicago Cubs.

Hank Greenberg played for the Tigers from 1933-1941, was in the military in 1942-1944 and rejoined the Tigers in 1945 and '46.

**By the time Hank reached home plate, he was caught up in a maelstrom of humanity that was every Tiger on the team.**

1944. They all were there.

Greenberg's four-run circuit smash into the leftfield stands came off Nelson Potter, ace of the Brownie mound staff.

"What kind of a pitch was it?" Greenberg asked afterward. "I really don't know. I think it was a high one. My big scare was that it might go foul."

The Tigers were trailing, 3-2, with one out and the bases clogged with eager runners who carried a trip into the 1945 World Series on their mud-laden spikes.

Hubby Walker, who batted for Hal Newhouser, started the big ninth-inning uprising with a single. Skeeter Webb bunted, and Walker slid through the mud and water to beat the throw to second. Red Borom went in to run for Walker.

Eddie Mayo laid down a bunt and both runners advanced. Potter issued an intentional pass to Doc Cramer, filling the bases. That placed the responsibility on the shoulders of Greenberg.

The count was one ball and one strike on Greenberg, the man who

came back from four years in the service of his country to play baseball.

Potter wound up and threw a high fast one toward the plate. Greenberg hit the ball on a line into the leftfield stands at the 351-foot mark to drive home Borom, Webb and Cramer.

By the time Greenberg reached home plate, he was caught up in a maelstrom of humanity that was every Tiger on the team.

He was hugged and roughed and kissed and pummeled.

It was 1940 all over again. That was the last time the Tigers won the AL pennant. They did it that year when Rudy York hit a two-run homer off Cleveland's Bob Feller to clinch the flag.

But they didn't have to do it under such adverse playing conditions. Storms had drenched the field for 10 straight days; the temperature was 57; only 5,582 fans were huddled in the dank park to see baseball history made by a man who hit his 13th home run since he came back from the wars last July 1.

Newhouser had replaced starter

Virgil Trucks, just three days out after 19 months in the Navy, in the sixth inning. Although the ace left-hander lost the lead Trucks had held, he rode to his 25th victory on Greenberg's homer.

Trucks pitched great ball until manager O'Neill jerked him with one out and Brownies on first and second in the sixth. Detroit led, 2-1, at the time after coming from behind to tie the score in the fifth and take its first lead in the top of the sixth.

The park was a dismal place.

A misty rain swept down from low-hanging clouds in such a fashion that the start was delayed 50 minutes.

After warming up a little bit here and a little more there, Trucks finally had a batter to pitch to. He blasted two strikes past Don Gutteridge, who then lined a double to right that promptly blossomed into a St. Louis run when Lou Finney, next up, singled to left.

That St. Louis run looked big as Potter retired the first six Tigers in order before serving a single to Jimmy Outlaw to open the third.

With two away in the fifth, Potter dished up a walk to Trucks and Webb sent him skittering around to third with a single over second.

Up came Mayo to send Trucks home and put Webb on third with another single.

The Tigers came through with the run in the sixth that gave them a lead. Roy Cullenbine walked and then made the smartest play of the game. When catcher Frank Mancuso went back to the screen to make a nice catch of York's pop foul for the second out, Cullenbine tagged up and barreled for second under full steam. He caught the Browns asleep, so they decided to walk Outlaw.

They did and Paul Richards drilled a single into center to send Cullenbine around third and across the plate with the run.

Webb threw out Lou Schulte, first batter in the sixth, but Potter then slashed a surprise double into left-center. When Gutteridge walked, O'Neill jerked Trucks and sent in Newhouser, who had trouble and walked Finney to load the bases with only one out. With a 3-2 count on Mark Christman, who hit for Milt Byrnes, Newhouser came across with a blazing fastball for a strikeout. Cramer then came through with a one-handed catch on George McQuinn's liner to preserve that one-run lead.

After doing so brilliantly in the sixth, Newhouser came out in the next frame and served two straight hits to the first two men to

DETROIT FREE PRESS

Greenberg, after hitting 13 homers in his war-shortened season, had two homers and seven RBIs in the World Series.

face him and bingo, just like that, the score was tied. Gene Moore doubled off the rightfield fence and Vern Stephens scored him with another hit that was held to a single by

Cullenbine's speedy fielding and fine throw-in. Newhouser then fanned the next two men and Webb threw out Potter.

The Browns then scored in the eighth and it looked

bad. After Gutteridge fanned, Finney singled. He was forced by Pete Gray, who scored when McQuinn doubled off the rightfield fence to make the score 3-2.

After doing so brilliantly in the sixth, Hal Newhouser came out in the next frame and served two straight hits to the first two men to face him and bingo, just like that, the score was tied.

NOT TILL THE FAT LADY SINGS **39**

**9**

THE SETUP:

It looked like the Pistons had finally conquered the Boston Garden ghosts. Just five seconds were left in Game 5 of the Eastern Conference finals. All the Pistons had to do was kill the clock. But Isiah Thomas tossed an ill-fated pass and ...

THE ELEMENTS

# Bird stole the ball!

BY JOHNETTE HOWARD

It was moments after what Pistons coach Chuck Daly called the "most bizarre" loss of his career. Now the Celtics' team trainer was giddily pushing the game-film cartridge into the VCR and playing the final five seconds over and over on the television inside the locker room.

"I was looking for a miracle and we got one," Boston guard Danny Ainge said moments after the Pistons gave away the game, 108-107, and the chance to move closer to the NBA Finals.

It evaporated like this: Isiah Thomas grabbing the ball from referee Jess Kersey and lobbing a pass to Bill Laimbeer eight feet to the left of Boston's basket with five seconds left. Celtics forward Larry Bird, cutting in front of Laimbeer and pawing

DETROIT FREE PRESS

One of the few blemishes on Isiah Thomas' legendary career with the Pistons happened in Game 5 of the 1987 Eastern Conference finals.

the ball down hard against the parquet floor, then shoveling a pass to Dennis Johnson as he streaked to the basket.

Then Johnson, ducking under leaping Pistons guard Joe Dumars, banked the ball off the glass and into

the basket with one second left, giving the Celtics a 3-2 lead in the best-of-seven Eastern Conference finals.

"I was going to foul Laimbeer, but the ball just kept staying in the air," Bird said. "They were all jumping around, celebrating at halfcourt. ... I saw I had a chance to steal it. No question they thought they had us, but you can't blame them. It was luck, no question about it."

To the Pistons, it was more than heartbreaking. When asked if he could describe what he felt as he ran to the basket, then leaped in the air in case Johnson's shot rolled out, Thomas breathed heavily and said: "No, I can't."

Daly said he was trying to call a time-out after Dennis Rodman blocked Bird's final shot and Rick Mahorn bounced the ball off Celtics guard Jerry Sichting's leg. But

---

**"I was looking for a miracle and we got one."**

**DANNY AINGE,** moments after Larry Bird stole the ball with five seconds left against the Pistons in Game 5 of the 1987 Eastern Conference finals

**40** FIRST TEAM

"They were all jumping around, celebrating at half-court. ... I saw I had a chance to steal it. No question they thought they had us, but you can't blame them. It was luck, no question about it."

**LARRY BIRD**, on his steal in Game 5 of the 1987 Eastern Conference finals

DETROIT FREE PRESS

> "You can say I should have called a time-out. You can say I should not have thrown the pass. You can say I should have thrown the ball harder or Bill should have come in. But all I can say is they stole the ball and they won the game."

**ISIAH THOMAS**, on Bird's steal

DETROIT FREE PRESS

Dennis Rodman was shaping up to be the hero of Game 5. He blocked Larry Bird's driving lay-up with five seconds left.

Thomas said, "I was aware there was a time-out left.

"But I didn't see anybody signaling for one, though, and I didn't feel the need to signal for one.

"I didn't see him (Bird). ... You can say I should have called a time-out. You can say I should not have thrown the pass. You can say I should have thrown the ball harder or Bill should have come in. But all I can say is they stole the ball and they won the game."

Despite Bird's 36 points, 12 rebounds and nine assists, the Celtics still seemed destined to lose. The Pistons led by five points twice early in the fourth quarter and, given the troubles center Robert Parish (sprained left ankle) and power forward Kevin McHale were having, it became clear with eight minutes to go that the game would boil down to whether Bird could lift the Celtics.

Parish limped off twice in the fourth quarter after spraining his ankle and word shot down press row with 3:41 remaining that he would not return. It didn't immedi-

Boston's Robert Parish got away, momentarily, with a sucker punch of the Pistons' Bill Laimbeer in Game 5. The refs didn't see it so nothing was called. But the league office noticed and Parish was suspended for Game 6, which the Pistons won.

DETROIT FREE PRESS

ately turn out badly for Boston. Reserve Darren Daye replaced Parish and scored the Celtics' next five points.

That gave Boston a 100-99 lead, but Daye fouled out with 2:21 remaining and the Celtics went to a three-guard lineup of Ainge, Johnson and Sichting.

The teams exchanged baskets until Mahorn grabbed a defensive rebound and, following a time-out, Thomas made a 15-foot jumper with 17 seconds left that gave the Pistons a 107-106 lead. It looked as if it would stand up when Bird's attempt to drive by Mahorn failed, thanks to Rodman's block.

Several Pistons were still leaping for joy when Bird sent the Garden's 14,890 fans rocketing to their feet with the steal and pass that, Celtics assistant coach Jimmy Rodgers said, "Memories are made of."

The loss was especially numbing since the Pistons have overcome so much to just be in a position to win the game. Laimbeer was making his first Garden appearance since being fined $5,000 for his takedown of Bird in Game 3, and everyone expected some heavy harassment. Laimbeer even invited some during pregame introductions by cupping his right hand

around his ear to suggest he couldn't hear the boos very well.

But the boos and treatment from the Garden fans weren't nearly as bad as the call referees Jack Madden and Kersey failed to make with 23 seconds left in the first half, when Parish clawed at Laimbeer's neck, then landed a short rabbit punch to the side of Laimbeer's face.

Laimbeer and Parish had turned to watch Thomas try to dribble away from Daye beneath the Celtics backboard. Parish, standing behind Laimbeer near the foul line, hit Laimbeer from behind and Laimbeer fell, clutching his face.

The foul was called on Daye and Parish was given neither a foul nor a technical — let alone the ejection the Pistons coaching staff demanded.

Thomas made one of two free throws, capping a 21-12 Pistons' run that Parish had helped fuel with two missed lay-ups and two turnovers. And the Pistons trailed, 58-56, at the half.

Both referees said they did not see the punch. Daly said he appealed to alternate referee Mike Mathis, who was seated at courtside, "But I could not get a reply. It was a flagrant foul," Daly said.

### INSIDE THE FINISH
## What made the end so exciting:
### BEASTS OF THE EAST

 There were other classics in the Pistons' playoff grudge matches with the Celtics in 1985-88. It took them three years to get past their Boston rivals.

### 1985 EASTERN CONFERENCE SEMIFINALS

Down 2-1 in the series, Vinnie Johnson hit 10 of 11 shots and scored 22 of his 34 points in the fourth, rallying the Pistons from an 11-point deficit to a 102-99 victory. Larry Bird, suffering from a sore elbow, recovered to score 43 points in Boston's 130-123 victory in Game 5. The Celtics closed the series with a 123-113 victory in Detroit.

PAULINE LUBENS/DETROIT FREE PRESS

The Pistons lost momentum when Vinnie Johnson, left, and Adrian Dantley got into a nasty collision that knocked both of them out of Game 7 in the Eastern finals.

### 1987 EASTERN CONFERENCE FINALS

 Adrian Dantley was hospitalized with a concussion and Vinnie Johnson sat out most of the fourth quarter of Game 7 after the two bumped heads. The Pistons lost, 117-114.

### 1988 EASTERN CONFERENCE FINALS

 The Pistons argued that Kevin McHale's three-pointer to send Game 2 into overtime was actually a two-pointer, but they lost the argument and the game, 119-115, in double overtime.

With the series 2-2, the Pistons went to Boston and rallied from a 16-point deficit to win Game 5, 102-96, in overtime. That was the beginning of the end for the Celtics, who were smothered in Game 6, 95-90.

DETROIT FREE PRESS

Vinnie Johnson, left, and Isiah Thomas share a tender moment after Detroit beat Boston in the East finals in 1988.

**THE DATE:** October 13, 1990

**THE LOCATION:** Michigan Stadium, Ann Arbor

**THE SETUP:**
Trailing the Spartans by one, top-ranked Michigan went for two points in the game's final seconds. U-M's Desmond Howard got his hands on the pass but dropped it after tangling with MSU's Eddie Brown. MSU won because of ...

# The imaginary reception

**BY STEVE KORNACKI**

You never know where Desmond (Magic) Howard will turn up.

There he was in the parking lot outside Michigan Stadium, rapping on the window of the Michigan State bus. The rest of the Wolverines were long gone, but Howard wanted to talk with his friend, Spartans offensive guard Roosevelt Wagner.

"That's just the way Magic is," said J.D. Howard, pointing at his son and smiling. "He plays hard and shows good sportsmanship. After a tough loss in high school, he went to the other locker room to congratulate them."

Now he was doing the same thing after losing, 28-27, to MSU.

Howard had been the central figure in the game, catching eight passes for 140 yards and returning a kickoff 95 yards for a touchdown. But everyone was talking about the play he didn't make — although he contended he did — on the two-point conversion attempt after U-M's last touchdown.

"I definitely had possession," Howard said. "But the official made the call. It was a no-call, actually."

Howard was grabbed by MSU cornerback Eddie Brown as he made a slant cut into the end zone, and he still caught the ball with both hands between his right shoulder pad and helmet. But Howard lost it as he crashed to the end zone on his back. He looked at back judge Ken Baker for the two-point signal, a penalty flag, anything.

But all that came was Baker's "wave-off" signal for an incompletion.

"I just want to get away with my family now," Howard said. "I want to have something to eat and talk with them, leave this behind."

His father and his mother, Hattie Dawkins, watched the game with his brother Jermaine, a junior football player at Cleveland (Ohio) St. Joseph.

"I almost had to dial 911," Hattie said. "That was too stressful. I lost my voice screaming. I thought Desmond would pull it out, and Michigan would get this game."

"I just knew that if it was anywhere in his hands, he would pull it in," J.D. said. "I just don't know. ... But I'll tell you what. I give (coach) Gary Moeller a lot of credit. When he came into St. Joseph and recruited Magic and

> "I definitely had possession. But the official made the call. It was a no-call, actually."
> **DESMOND HOWARD**, in the aftermath of the controversial play involving he and MSU's Eddie Brown

"THAT PLAY SEEMS SO FAR AWAY NOW. SO FAR AWAY."

JULIAN H. GONZALEZ/DETROIT FREE PRESS

**DESMOND HOWARD**, on his 95-yard kickoff return for a touchdown late in the fourth quarter

"He pushed me first, but I pushed him second. And it's always the second guy who gets caught. I thought maybe I'd see a flag. When I didn't, I got up and headed for the sidelines as fast as I could."

**EDDIE BROWN**, on whether he interfered with Desmond Howard on the two-point conversion

JULIAN H. GONZALEZ/DETROIT FREE PRESS

Michigan State got state bragging rights over rival Michigan after upsetting the No. 1-ranked Wolverines in Ann Arbor.

Elvis, he said he had confidence in them. Moeller showed true confidence in this game. He kept letting them throw."

Elvis Grbac completed 17 of 32 passes for 213 yards and two touchdowns.

U-M hadn't thrown more since Jim Harbaugh had 37 attempts in a 1984 loss to Washington. Grbac also threw two interceptions — one on the final "Hail Mary" pass after Vada Murray

recovered an onside kick — and seven of his passes were dropped.

The game was up for grabs in the fourth quarter: Each side scored two touchdowns in the final 6:03.

So much happened that Howard's 95-yard touchdown return with 5:50 left was barely discussed afterward.

"That play seems so far away now," Howard said. "So far away."

He looked into the night outside Michigan Stadium. There were no

cheering fans, no replays. Just the three MSU chartered buses waiting to pull out, and his family by his side.

His parents are divorced, and his mother remarried. But football Saturdays bring them together again to sit on the 50 and cheer for their son.

Howard wears his father's initials on his wrist tape for inspiration, and J.D. wears his pride for his son on his sleeve.

"We call him Magic more than Desmond," J.D. said, beaming.

And why shouldn't they? Their son is an electric player, blending toughness and determination with flash and speed.

"I was jumping up and down on the 95-yard touchdown," said Hattie. "I was hollering and screaming, 'That's my baby! Watch him run.'"

Howard caught the kickoff at the middle of the field, on the 5-yard line, and ran left as a four-man wall provided maneuvering room. He eluded a diving Spartan at the 27 and was untouched as he darted to the sideline at midfield.

Several Wolverines ran interference and cut off the angles on the final defenders. That's where Howard's running ability took over.

He was a tailback at St. Joseph, and the timing on his cutback at the MSU 40 was perfect. Myron Bell dove and missed him there, and kicker John Langeloh had no hope of catching the blur.

"Once I cut back, I knew I was gone," Howard said.

It was strange hearing him describe such a dramatic run with absolutely no emotion.

"We just have to live with that call and go on," he said.

No matter what the conversation turned to, it always returned to the failed conversion. It was the play U-M needed to retain its No. 1 ranking in the polls, and the one that got away.

Referee John Nealon explained the call: "The conversing officials just didn't see it as an interference-type situation. It looked to me like he never really had possession of the thing. He hits the ground and it's coming out."

So what we are saying is he didn't have possession.

"In order to have possession, you have to be able to do one of three things: to run with it, hold it, kick it, whatever."

Kick it?

Well, after all, the Wolverines did claim the call was booted. Moeller shook his head upon leaving the interview room and uttered, "Ridiculous!"

Brown, the cornerback in question, said, "He pushed me first, but I pushed him second. And it's always the second guy who gets caught. I thought maybe I'd see a flag. When I didn't, I got up and headed for the sidelines as fast as I could."

As the MSU buses drove away, and the Howards walked to their car, only one thing was certain:

MSU 28, U-M 27.

## INSIDE THE FINISH
# What made the end so exciting:
### YOU HEARD IT FIRST

 Here's the WWJ-AM (950) radio call of Michigan's failed two-point conversion attempt with six seconds left in the 28-27 loss to Michigan State:

JULIAN H. GONZALEZ/DETROIT FREE PRESS

Broadcaster Jim Brandstatter was the bearer of bad news for U-M fans in 1990.

DALE CONQUEST: (Gary) Moeller has made his decision.
JIM BRANDSTATTER: He's going to go for the victory.
CONQUEST: Oh, what a gutsy call.
BRANDSTATTER: You bet.
CONQUEST: The snap, (Elvis) Grbac drops, throws for the end zone to Howard — makes the catch!! Michigan gets the two-point conversion!
BRANDSTATTER: No, he dropped the ball!
CONQUEST: Apparently he dropped it when he hit the ground.
BRANDSTATTER: I'll tell you what else, there was interference on the play. ... Howard gets inside, and he is tackled in the end zone, tackled in the end zone by the defensive back and there's no call. .... There's no question that the ball came out. The problem is the Michigan State back, Eddie Brown, tackled him. ... Well, there you go.

### THE AFTERMATH

Michigan State coach George Perles objected to an admission by the Big Ten supervisor of football officials that a mistake was made on Michigan's two-point conversion attempt.

David Parry, the supervisor, said officials erred by not calling pass interference against the Spartans.

"I'm a little disappointed we'd have anybody go public from our league office," Perles said. "I'm sure the commissioner (Jim Delany) will get into it and see that we don't do our wash in the street.

"Keep talking about it. Keep talking about it. I don't think it's exactly class. Call the commissioner and find out if it's policy."

HUGH GRANNUM/DETROIT FREE PRESS

MSU running back Hyland Hickson ran for 90 yards and scored on a 26-yard run.

# Second team

**THE LINEUP**

**11**

A goal worth
waiting for

**12**

Brown Bomber's
crash landing

**13**

Bringing down
The House

**14**

21 points in
2 minutes

**15**

Phantom
buzzer-beater

"It's the kind of goal every player dreams about scoring in his career. Including me."

**STEVE YZERMAN**, on his 55-foot slap shot in overtime of Game 7 of the 1996 Western Conference semifinals

**THE ELEMENTS**
Look for these eight elements in each of the 50 thrilling finishes:

**THE BIG COLLAPSE**

**THE BIG COMEBACK**

**CONTROVERSY STRIKES**

**THE HEART-BREAKER**

**HIGH STAKES**

**INDIVIDUAL EFFORT**

**VS**
**THE BIG RIVALRY**

**TEAM EFFORT**

**16** The Great Clock-troversy

**17** Pure gold

**18** Crank up the A.C.

**19** Delayed gratification

**20** A painful lesson

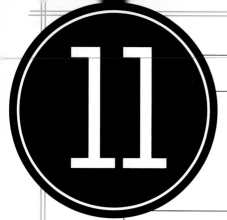

**THE DATE:** May 16, 1996

**THE LOCATION:** Joe Louis Arena, Detroit

**THE SETUP:**
In Game 7 of the Western semis, the Wings and the Blues played 80 minutes of scoreless hockey. Chris Osgood and Jon Casey stopped shot after shot. Finally, at 1:15 of the second overtime, Stevie Y uncorked a 55-footer and scored ...

# A goal worth waiting for

### By MITCH ALBOM

It was every suspense film you have ever watched, every thriller you have ever read, every nervous waiting room you have ever sat in, all rolled into one nail-biting, double-overtime evening at Joe Louis Arena, 19,000 exhausted fans, tapping their chests at every break to make sure the old ticker was still working.

And, finally, a few minutes before midnight, the smiling doctor emerged with the good news:

It's a goal!

"YES! YES! YES!" the fans screamed, when Steve Yzerman put an end to the most dramatic playoff game in Detroit in years, whacking a 55-foot shot past the seemingly impenetrable Jon Casey 1:15 into the second overtime to win Game 7 of this second-round playoff series, 1-0.

The crowd erupted like an uncorked volcano, and Yzerman himself was lifted into the air by the force of his own exuberance, running and cheering as his skates never touched the ice.

It's a goal!

Breathe again.

"I don't usually score that way," Yzerman said sheepishly, after the goal that ended this agonizing series, one in which the Wings blew a lead, nearly fell off the cliff and fought back to take the final two games.

"It's the kind of goal every player dreams about in his career. Including me."

"Had you ever scored in double-overtime before?" he was asked.

"Never," he said.

"Did you get the puck?"

He smiled. "I got the puck."

Well. How could he not? What a finish! What a perfect end! A night that desperately called for a hero got the call from the perfect cast member, the captain himself, a guy who has been waiting for this night longer than anyone on the roster, and has been playing as if the last lights of his life hung in the scoreboard.

Even the opposing coach, Mike Keenan, called him "the best player in the series." And just seconds before his miracle goal, he'd set up a perfect chance for teammate Sergei Fedorov, putting the puck in front of the net. But Fedorov slapped it into Casey and was denied, as were 38 shots before his.

Yzerman figured, "do it yourself."

A few seconds later, he did, whacking a high, stinging shot that hit the

> **"It's the kind of goal every player dreams about in his career. Including me."**
>
> **STEVE YZERMAN**, on scoring the series-winning goal from 55 feet away

## "I DON'T USUALLY SCORE THAT WAY."

**STEVE YZERMAN**, on his series-winning slap shot in double overtime

Hockeytown collectively exhaled after Steve Yzerman touched off this celebration in Game 7 of the second round of the 1996 playoffs.

"Hon-estly? I thought, 'It went in? No way!'"

**STEVE YZERMAN**, on the improba-bility of his game-winner

crossbar with a "ping" and fell in behind a startled Casey.

It's a goal!

Breathe again.

"Anyone who doubted the character of this team should think again after tonight," said forward Kris Draper, smiling among his happy but exhausted teammates in the Wings' locker room.

Indeed, it was a game teams that want championships have to win. It began frantically, with the Wings playing like soldiers on their first day in combat, shooting at anything that moves. The crowd rose and roared with each attack, expecting perhaps a high-scoring finale. But even though the Wings chalked up 14 shots to the Blues' four, few were quality efforts, and those few were

weakly hit or just a fraction of a sec-ond too late to beat Casey.

Igor Larionov came close, hitting a post, and Yzerman had a chance at a puck that Casey lost sight of, but the goalie found it before the captain did. The period ended scoreless, and one chunk of someone's last evening of the season was over.

The second period, for Detroit fans, was like the second stage of torture. The Wings did everything but pick up the building and tilt the puck in. They pressured, banged, fought in corners, whacked shots and whacked rebounds, and the moment the puck came out of the St. Louis end, they went and took it back and came storming in again.

There was a stretch where some of Detroit's grittier and less famous

names — Martin Lapointe, Marc Bergevin — joined Slava Kozlov and Keith Primeau in a desperate and magnificent surge, for a solid minute they were keeping the puck in the St. Louis end, slamming everything, fir-ing, reloading, firing again, and the crowd rose spontaneously to its feet, cheering the effort. If trying hard could win a championship, it would have been over at that moment.

So by the time the third period began, the score was 0-0, but it was not a tie game. The Blues seemed lighter, and the Wings were weighed down by expectations. I have always believed that Joe Louis Arena is as much a hindrance as a help in the playoffs. You can feel the 41 years of disappointment on every close play. It's like skating around with a pack of rocks on your back. This might explain why the Wings had lost two Game 7s in the last three years — both at home.

But these are not your old Wings.

"This was as relaxed an overtime game as I can remember playing, as far as the players were concerned," Yzerman said. "We just felt we were going to win, and we said, 'Come on, let's get it done.'"

When in doubt, go to the captain, right?

Now, the purist will say the Wings should never have been in this position, that the Blues were a sub-.500 team with an aging superstar (Wayne Gretzky) that didn't have any business dangling the Wings over the edge of a cliff. And they are right — from a purist point of view. But what in life works so purely?

The fact is, sometimes things go wrong, and sometimes things go right, and sometimes things go right but take an awfully long time to do so. A few very important things came out of this long series: 1) The Wings know what it's like to hang over the edge and pull themselves back up. 2) Chris Osgood is officially The Goalie — and officially a hot goalie. And 3) Yzerman, the captain, has moved up a notch to the level of Gretzky, Mario Lemieux and others; namely, he's the guy to lead the way when the biggest games are on the line. In years past, he hasn't always had the chance, sometimes because of injuries, sometimes because the Wings were eliminated too quickly.

No doubts now. They disappeared with his two goals in Game 2, his hat trick in Game 3 and his closing number just before midnight, the pinging shot heard around the hockey world.

MARY SCHROEDER/DETROIT FREE PRESS

Chris Osgood triumphed over St. Louis' Jon Casey in a battle of goalies. Osgood would have to wait until 1998 to bask in the glory as the starter of a Stanley Cup winner.

A word about the Blues, who seemed to find themselves late last week, in the overtime period of Game 3, when Igor Kravchuk intercepted a clearing pass and smacked the puck past Mike Vernon for the victory. "How about that?" they seemed to say. "We can beat these guys."

Before that, they were members of the chorus; after that, they were stars of the show. And in Game 7, when they could have skated out and fallen over, they stood tall. They fought off the Wings' attack and made the building shake every time they had a shot on goal.

Ah, well, the Blues are history now. Remember the words of Yzerman, the captain, before Game 7. He encouraged the fans — as well as his teammates — to keep in mind this is a sport, and to "relax and have fun."

Once we start breathing again, we can do that.

"What were you thinking the moment you saw that red light go on?" Yzerman was asked.

"Honestly?" he answered. "I thought, 'It went in? No way!'"

**INSIDE THE FINISH**

## What made the end so exciting:

### DOUBLING UP IN DOUBLE OVERTIME

Stevie Y's not the only guy with a playoff double-OT game-winner. Brendan Shanahan picked up one in both the 1997 and 1998 Stanley Cup runs.

**1997: WESTERN CONFERENCE SEMIFINALS VS. ANAHEIM, GAME 4**

ANAHEIM, Calif. — While you were sleeping, Brendan Shanahan scored 17:03 into double overtime, giving the Wings a 3-2 victory, a four-game sweep of the Mighty Ducks and a spot in the Western finals for the third straight season. Shanahan finally ended the affair at 3:27 a.m. Detroit time, about five hours after it had started. A large group celebrated around Shanahan near the Ducks' goal and a smaller pack swarmed Wings goalie Mike Vernon at the opposite end.

**1998: WESTERN CONFERENCE SEMIFINALS VS. ST. LOUIS, GAME 3**

ST. LOUIS — Another Western Conference semifinal game, another game-winner for Brendan Shanahan, who ended the game with 8:48 left in the second overtime, sliding the puck through Grant Fuhr for a 3-2 Wings victory.

"If it was a breakaway I might have gotten down in a fetal position on the ice and sucked my thumb," Shanahan said of his game-winner. "I didn't even have time to think."

**12**

**THE SETUP:**
Max Schmeling came into his first bout with Joe Louis a huge underdog. But the big German was no bum. He didn't believe the hype surrounding the huge puncher from Detroit. He delivered a KO. It was the ...

THE ELEMENTS

# Brown Bomber's crash landing

### By W.W. EDGAR

The lightning struck at Yankee Stadium, but not where it was expected to.

It came in the form of a slashing right hand that Max Schmeling landed on Joe Louis' chin midway in the 12th round and toppled the man they thought was invincible to the canvas for the full count.

When the blow landed and the Brown Bomber staggered along the ropes and then fell to his knees, the gathering that numbered close to 40,000 became eyewitnesses to the greatest upset in the history of boxing.

From the middle of the fourth round when Louis was dropped for no count by a short, choppy right, until the lightning struck in the 12th, Louis was badly beaten and a far cry from the Bomber who had crashed his way from the amateurs to the rank of leading challenger for the heavyweight title in two short years.

When the fighters entered the arena, Schmeling was considered the condemned man of the ring. No one in the vast throng conceded him a chance to survive more than three rounds, and you could have named your own odds that he would win. But less than an hour later, he had slain his executioner and marched along to earn a title bout with Jimmy Braddock, an ambition Schmeling claimed would serve as the inspiration to carry him to victory when the match was signed.

The fight was earned by Schmeling when he toppled Louis and left him a broke and battered bulk two minutes and 29 seconds after the 12th round started.

The perfect fighting machine of the age proved anything but that shortly after the bell rang when he walked out to face the German who was attempting a comeback. Before the echo of the opening bell had faded into the chilly night, Louis had been staggered by a right hand that landed flush on his chin and made him wince.

Little thought was given to this at the time when he came right back to beat a tattoo of left jabs on Schmeling's features that left them crimson. But shortly before the round ended, Schmeling landed another right and the Bomber went

---

*"Ach. I knew I would do it. Everyone think I would be like (Primo) Carnera, (King) Levinsky, (Max) Baer and (Paulino) Uzcudun, but I knew I wouldn't, I knew I could lick him ..."*

**MAX SCHMELING**, on his upset of heavyweight champion and Detroiter Joe Louis in 1936

When the fighters entered the arena, Schmeling was considered the condemned man of the ring. No one in the vast throng conceded him a chance to survive more than three rounds, and you could have named your own odds that he would win.

In their 1938 rematch, Joe Louis put Max Schmeling down in the first round. Schmeling's corner tossed in the towel after 1:24.

back on his heels.

That was the first sign that he was in trouble. The handwriting became plainly discernible midway in the second when another short, choppy right caused Louis to stagger.

The setting for the finish began to take definite form with the start of the third round. Louis staggered out of the corner on rubbery legs and walked right into a solid right that landed on the side of his jaw, staggering him again.

The die was cast a minute after the fourth round started when a short, choppy right dumped the Bomber on the floor for no count. He leaped to his feet immediately, but he was in bad shape and Schmeling missed a knockout only because he failed to follow up the advantage.

Only once after that was Schmeling in danger, and that was in the sixth when Louis crashed a hard right to his rival's head. Schmeling fell back on his heels for a second and Louis' face writhed in pain. It was feared he had broken his hand, for he seldom used it after that.

Schmeling had paced himself beautifully, and he came up fresh for the 12th. In contrast, Louis was dog-tired, scarcely could see out of his left eye, and only pecked with his fists in feeble attempts to erect a defense. No longer was he able to punch.

As he backed into Schmeling's corner, Schmeling lashed out his right and it landed squarely on the button. Louis went back on his heels and his arms dropped to his sides. It was evident that the climax was at hand. Louis, badly battered and reeling, fell back into the ropes and Schmeling followed in hot pursuit. The Brown Bomber was helpless as he stood like a tree in a windstorm and offered no resistance.

One, two, three, four right-hand smashes landed on his chin and he started to sink. The fifth, carrying

all his power in the smiling German's body, spun Louis around, his face to the crowd, and he slumped to his knees, a pitiful sight as his hands hung limply over the middle strand of the rope.

At the count of four he toppled over on his face, his nose buried deep in the rosin, while Johnny McAvoy, the knockdown timekeeper and referee Arthur Donovan, in unison toiled off the fatal 10-second count.

Schmeling leaped with joy and then ran over to help carry the beaten Bomber to his corner.

His handlers worked frantically on him for five minutes, but Louis was still in a daze. He didn't know what had struck him, and it wasn't fully 10 minutes before he left the ring.

And when he left, battered and bruised, he left behind a chance to meet Braddock for the heavyweight title. All arrangements had been made to sign him for the match, so confident were his handlers that he would conquer Schmeling. They had hoped to guide Louis to the championship of the world and allow him to become the first black man since Jack Johnson to hold the title. But these hopes faded and the Bomber will have to start again at the bottom of the ladder.

Back in the dressing room, Louis still was dazed. He claimed he did not know a thing after the fourth round, when he was knocked down. The German leaped for joy in his dressing room and in rich German accent said, "Ach. I knew I would do it. Everyone think I would be like (Primo) Carnera, (King) Levinsky, (Max) Baer and (Paulino) Uzcudun, but I knew I wouldn't, I knew I could lick him …"

He surely did earn a chance at the title. For he turned in a masterful job and proved beyond all doubt that Louis, who was looked upon as an invincible fighting machine, was human after all.

## INSIDE THE FINISH
## What made the end so exciting:

JOE LOUIS MEMORIAL VIDEO ROOM

Joe Louis, pictured with Max Schmeling before their 1938 rematch, was the pride of America, particularly for black Detroiters. "He was our hope," said Dorothy Mann, a friend of Louis.

### DETROIT PARTIES AFTER THE REMATCH

**VS** It was a celebration like none other.

That's how Dorothy Mann, a friend of Joe Louis, remembers Detroit's jubilation after Louis beat Max Schmeling in a rematch for the world heavyweight championship on June 22, 1938.

Mann listened on the radio with others in Paradise Valley, the entertainment district in the Black Bottom neighborhood, the cultural and economic center of black Detroit.

"As soon as it was announced that he knocked him out, it was an explosion in this city as people screamed and hollered from their porches," Mann said. "I don't think anything has ever equaled it since or before."

The Bronx bout had huge political and racial implications. Schmeling was cast as a representative of Nazi Germany. Louis was a black American. Before the fight, Louis was invited to the White House, where President Franklin D. Roosevelt told him he wanted him to win.

Louis did, in a first-round knockout, retaining the title.

The Free Press recounted the Paradise Valley celebration this way: "Cheering, shouting, singing and above all dancing, a crowd estimated at 10,000 gaily cavorted in the streets after the fight, in the first organized demonstration since Louis has become world champion."

Adolf Hitler had claimed that Schmeling's 1936 victory over Louis was proof that the white race was superior.

"I think there would have been mass suicides throughout the United States" if Louis had lost again, Mann said. "He was our hope. He was everything we could dream that a person of color could be."

Louis' niece, Helen Wilhite of Detroit, was 7 at the time of the fight. "I've seen pictures where the people were laughing and dancing and having a good time, grateful that Joe had done what he said he could do," Wilhite said.

By George Sipple

THE DATE: September 24, 1994

THE LOCATION: Michigan Stadium, Ann Arbor

THE SETUP:

It was early, but Michigan was aiming for a title. With the Buffaloes down to one play deep in their own territory, it looked as if the run would continue. But CU's Kordell Stewart heaved up a 64-yard prayer to Michael Westbrook that ended up .

THE ELEMENTS

# Bringing down The House

BY STEVE KORNACKI

JULIAN H. GONZALEZ/DETROIT FREE PRESS

Although Kordell Stewart's Hail Mary was a 64-yard pass, when he threw it, he was standing on his 27. The pass was deflected at U-M's 2.

It was minutes before the scoreboard operator at Michigan Stadium could bring himself to flick the visitors' final six points onto the scoreboard: COLORADO 27, MICHIGAN 26.

The U-M fans in the crowd of 106,427 stood stunned as if awaiting another miracle. But Kordell Stewart's 64-yard touchdown pass to Michael Westbrook with no time remaining was all she wrote.

The game and a chance for an undefeated season ended for U-M.

"My heart can't be broken," a Wolverines fan said as he left the stadium.

"I'm conditioned for this."

It was the third time in six seasons that U-M lost a home game it had all but tucked in its back pocket.

In 1988, the Wolverines led Miami, 30-14, in the fourth quarter, only to be riddled by quarterback Steve Walsh and lose, 31-30, as the Hurricanes scored 17 points in the final 5:23.

Illinois' Johnny Johnson fired the heartbreaker last year, a 15-yard touchdown pass to Jim Klein on fourth down with 41 seconds left for a 24-21 win. U-M had that one packed away until Ricky Powers fumbled with his team in position to run out the clock.

Now add the Colorado comeback to the list.

And still, of Wolverines players or coaches asked to choose whether Illinois or Colorado hurt more, only quarterback Todd Collins said losing to the Illini was tougher.

"We're all thinking of a play we want back. This is a hard one to choke down."

JAY RIEMERSMA, Michigan tight end, on the feeling among the Wolverines after losing on a last-second Hail Mary

"I WAS DOWN THERE AND SHOULD'VE MADE THE PLAY, BUT IT DIDN'T HAPPEN. I HAD IT IN MY HANDS."

**CHUCK WINTERS**, Michigan free safety, on giving up a Hail Mary catch to boyhood friend Michael Westbrook

DOUGLAS KANTER/ASSOCIATED PRESS

"Shoot, this is way harder than any loss. We practically dominated the second half, and this was a crappy way to lose."

**BOBBY POWERS**, Michigan inside linebacker, on his emotions after the loss

JULIAN H. GONZALEZ/DETROIT FREE PRESS

After catching Kordell Stewart's pass, The Big House belonged to Michael Westbrook and a caravan of Buffaloes fans.

The game against the Buffaloes was for big stakes, though. If the Wolverines were to complete an undefeated season against what the NCAA rated the nation's toughest schedule, it would have been tough to deny them the national title.

"We had a chance at a great start and already saw this one as a 'W,'" offensive line coach Les Miles said.

"We would've carried a lot of momentum into the Big Ten season.

"I don't know when we've had a more painful loss. There were Rose Bowl ramifications against Illinois

## INSIDE THE FINISH

# What made the end so exciting:

### DOWN TO THE FINAL PLAY

The Hail Mary loss to Colorado was Michigan's seventh game decided on the final play; they added an eighth the next season. The Wolverines are 4-4 in those games, and 1-1 in games decided by more than a field goal on the final play. Here's the eight Michigan cliffhangers:

|  |  |  |  |  |  |  |  |
|---|---|---|---|---|---|---|---|
| OCTOBER 27, 1979 | SEPTEMBER 20, 1980 | OCTOBER 19, 1985 | OCTOBER 18, 1986 | NOVEMBER 15, 1986 | NOVEMBER 24, 1990 | SEPTEMBER 24, 1994 | AUGUST 26, 1995 |
| **MICHIGAN 27, INDIANA 21** | **NOTRE DAME 29, MICHIGAN 27** | **IOWA 12, MICHIGAN 10** | **MICHIGAN 20, IOWA 17** | **MINNESOTA 20, MICHIGAN 17** | **MICHIGAN 16, OHIO STATE 13** | **COLORADO 27, MICHIGAN 26** | **MICHIGAN 18, VIRGINIA 17** |
| 5-11 freshman wide receiver Anthony Carter catches a 45-yard touchdown pass from John Wangler, capping a 51-second, 78-yard drive to break a late tie with Indiana. | Harry Oliver boots a 51-yard field goal for the No. 8 Irish that just clears the goalposts in South Bend after No. 14 Michigan failed to make a 2-point conversion with 41 seconds left. | Rob Houghtlin makes his fourth field goal of the day — a 29-yarder — as time expires to put No. 1 Iowa ahead of No. 2 Michigan in Iowa City. | Just less than a year later, the No. 4 Wolverines get their revenge against the Hawkeyes when Mike Gillette hits a 34-yard field goal to stop No. 8 Iowa. | Chip Lohmiller gives Minnesota — 5-4 at the time with losses to MSU, OSU and Oklahoma by a total of 128 points — the Little Brown Jug with a 30-yard field goal against the No. 2 Wolverines. | Needing a win to go to the Rose Bowl, OSU coach John Cooper goes for it on 4th-and one from his own 29 with 38 seconds left. The Buckeyes are stuffed, and J.D. Carlson hits the game-winner from 37 yards out. | Needing a miracle, Colorado QB Kordell Stewart throws up a Hail Mary from 64 yards away; Detroit native Michael Westbrook comes down with the touchdown in The Big House. | The No. 14 Wolverines survive a scare in their season opener when Scott Dreisbach finds Mercury Hayes on a fourth-down, 15-yard pass to stop the No. 17 Cavaliers. |

last year, but this year we had a lot more going long-range."

Free safety Chuck Winters didn't hesitate with his decision: "This one was harder. I was down there and should've made the play, but it didn't happen. I had it in my hands."

Winters said he was coming down with the ball near the goal line, when receiver Blake Anderson punched it out. Westbrook stretched out and grabbed his destiny.

The NCAA has recorded games decided on final plays since 1971, and U-M has been involved in seven. But this was the first time it lost one of those outcomes on anything but a field goal.

Defeat had never before come with no warning, no time left.

"Shoot, this is way harder than any loss," inside linebacker Bobby Powers said. "We practically dominated the second half, and this was a crappy way to lose."

Amani Toomer could've been the highlight man with a 65-yard TD pass from Collins. Now it didn't matter.

Toomer said that even coach Gary Moeller's postgame speech was a blur. "I was too busy with my head down to hear," Toomer said.

"We're all thinking of a play we want back," tight end Jay Riemersma said.

"This is a hard one to choke down."

Moeller was frustrated at his postgame news conference, but kept his voice down until leaving the Crisler Arena lounge. But while waiting to do his postgame radio show in the adjoining hallway, he blurted out, "We can't sit back there and do that sloppy crap!"

Maybe he was referring to the Hail Mary pass or Che' Foster's fourth-quarter fumble. Maybe it was the offside call that doomed the last drive.

There was plenty to regret after this one, but no way to change it.

Winters sought out Westbrook before the Colorado bus pulled away. They clasped hands and hugged before nodding quickly and going their separate ways.

They had been Little League teammates in Detroit for a 13-year-old team called the Yankees, and now they had been reunited on a play that will be recalled until they are old and gray.

It was a game that got away from the Wolverines, but will never go away.

**14**

THE DATE: December 22, 1957

THE LOCATION: Kezar Stadium, San Francisco

THE SETUP:
En route to the most recent of their four NFL titles, the Lions face the 49ers in the Western final. Y.A. Tittle riddles Detroit with precise passing, and the Niners have a 20-point lead early in the third. But then the Lions roar back, scoring ...

THE ELEMENTS

# 21 points in 2 minutes

BY BOB LATSHAW

It's unbelievable, but the Lions are Western Division champions — the hard way.

In a season of fantastic finishes, the Lions got a melodramatic windup to nip the San Francisco 49ers, 31-27, before nearly 60,000 fans in Kezar Stadium.

Their triumph, their ninth against four defeats for the season, puts them into the championship game against the Cleveland Browns in Briggs Stadium.

With his team hobbled by injuries to most of the running backs, Detroit coach George Wilson picked Tom Tracy off the bench to score two touchdowns in 61 seconds and spark one of the greatest comebacks in NFL history.

Actually, the Lions scored three touchdowns in less than two minutes to pull this title out of the fire after trailing, 24-7, at the intermission.

The Lions didn't start to operate until virtually everybody figured the 49ers had the title all but salted away.

San Francisco took the kickoff to open the second half and marched deep into Detroit territory. Gordy Soltau's second field goal of the game, 2:22 into the third quarter, boosted the lead to 27-7.

No one, even the most rabid Detroit fan, thought those would be the last points of the year for the 49ers.

Detroit's defense came to life with a bang. Riddled by Y.A. Tittle's passes in the first half, the Lions roared through and around the 49ers.

Meanwhile, the Lions found a new

spark on offense, too — Tom (The Bomb) Tracy. Bob Long started the fireworks when he fell on Tittle's fumble on the 49ers' 27.

Nine plays later, Tracy hit left tackle for the first touchdown, a one-yard run.

The 49ers were forced to punt after four plays, and Detroit was off and running again from its 41.

This time Tracy had farther to go, but he did it almost as quickly. He squirted through a hole at right tackle, cut back, picked up a convoy of blockers and scampered into the 49ers end zone for a 58-yard score.

The two tallies came 61 seconds apart.

Again, the defense held the 49ers. And on the Lions' fifth play of a drive that started on their 46, Gene Gedman flashed into the end zone to

**In the closing moments Y.A. Tittle was still pitching, but Roger Zatkoff intercepted to give the Lions the ball again, and quarterback Tobin Rote killed the clock with three running plays.**

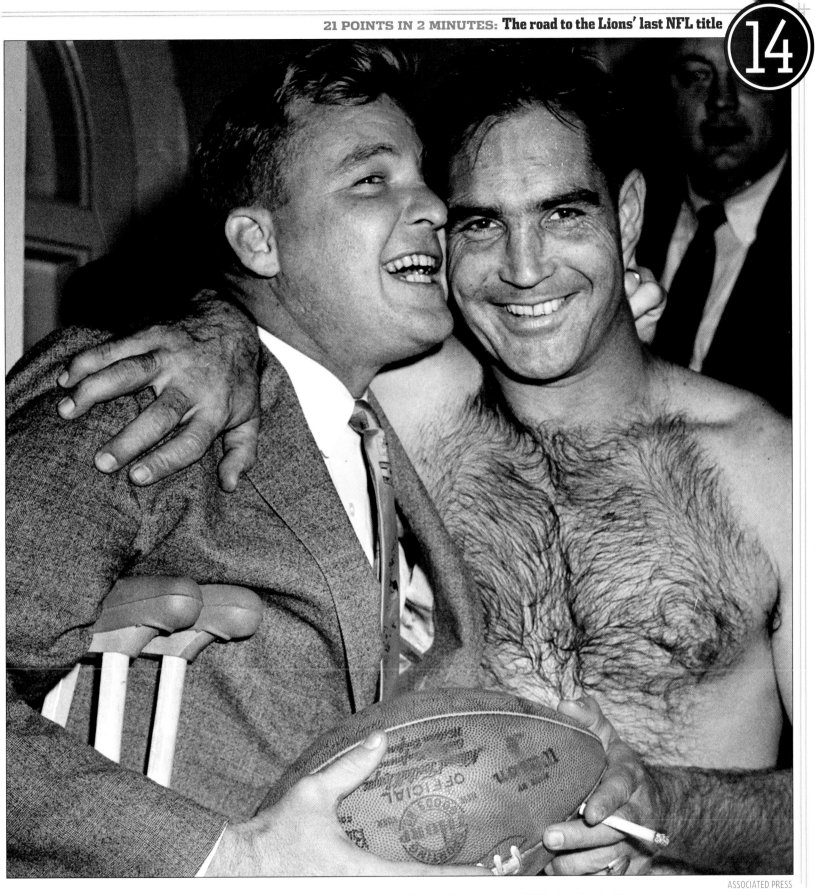

Bobby Layne, left, mugs for the cameras with backup Tobin Rote after the Lions rallied to defeat San Francisco in the 1957 Western Division title game.

"I only hope they've used all their heroics. If you'll excuse me now, I think I'll hurry back to Cleveland. I have a few things to tell Coach Paul Brown."

**PAUL BIXLER**, assistant coach on the Browns, who the Lions later defeated in the NFL title game, 59-14.

DETROIT FREE PRESS

Lions coach George Wilson, chatting with Free Press sports writer George Puscas, won the NFL title in 1957, his first season as coach in Detroit.

score from two yards out.

When Jim Martin kicked his fourth extra point, the Lions were out in front to stay, 28-27.

The game still had better than 14 minutes left, and those remaining minutes were jammed with drama. The defense provided most of the punch for the Lions fans during the frantic fourth quarter.

Gil Mains recovered a Joe Perry fumble to give the Lions a chance to pad their lead. Carl Karilivacz later intercepted a Tittle pass that provided another chance, but Tracy's fum-

ble on the goal line ended the threat.

Joe Schmidt then intercepted another Tittle pass, and Martin turned that one into three points and Detroit's final margin.

In the closing moments Tittle was still pitching, but Roger Zatkoff intercepted to give the Lions the ball again, and quarterback Tobin Rote killed the clock with three running plays.

That capped the great comeback. The defense that could do nothing right in the first half made its own breaks in the second 30 minutes.

The offense found weaknesses in the 49ers defense that wouldn't be dented in the first two quarters.

During this first 30 minutes, Tittle staged as brilliant a display of passing as you would want to see. He had lots of help from good protection and three fine receivers who had little trouble eluding the Lions secondary.

After keeping the Lions bottled up deep in their own territory, the 49ers gained possession on their own 42. This was one time they didn't score, but Bill Jessup punted the ball out of bounds on the Detroit 9, putting the

Lions in trouble.

When John Johnson fumbled two plays later, the Lions were in deeper trouble. The 49ers recovered the bobble on the Lions 21. A penalty moved the ball back to the 35, but that didn't bother Tittle.

After a screen pass failed to gain, Tittle found R.C. Owens on the goal line and lofted the usual high pass. Jimmy David couldn't outjump the lanky end, and the 49ers had their first touchdown.

Detroit had the ball for only four plays after the kickoff and one of these was a punt that wound up on the 49ers 41. It took just three plays for Tittle to score.

He hit Billy Wilson for a first down on the Detroit 47, and on the next play he clicked with Hugh McElhenny for the score.

With the 49ers leading, 14-0, the Lions showed their only spark of the first half, driving 61 yards in eight plays to score. Rote hit Dave Middleton, Jim Doran and Middleton again to move to the 49ers 7-yard line.

Two passes fell incomplete, however, and things didn't look too good. Howard Cassady then hit the line to the 3, and Rote found Steve Junker in the end zone with a perfect pass.

It took the 49ers 19 plays to get that one back after the kickoff. This time Tittle kept the 49ers on the ground most of the way, but he managed to click on key passes, three of them to Wilson on third down.

The big break in the drive, however, came when the officials ruled interference on Yale Lary. The penalty gave the 49ers a first down on the Detroit 18, and from there they managed to score six plays later.

This time Wilson was the scoring choice; he made a fine leaping catch in the end zone after he had beaten the defense. Soltau kicked his third extra point and the Lions were two touchdowns back again.

San Francisco increased its margin a few minutes later when Rote fumbled when he was hit by Matt Hazeltine and the 49ers recovered on the Detroit 41.

This time they had to settle for a field goal, however, when the defensive line dug in and stopped the attack at the 17.

Soltau kicked his three-pointer from the 25, and the 49ers went to the dressing room with a 24-7 lead.

Tittle, who completed 12 of 19 passes in the first half, finished the game 18-for-31. Rote was 16-for-30 for 214 yards and only one touchdown, but his key passes kept the second-half drives rolling.

Tracy was the game's top rusher, picking up 86 yards in 11 carries. McElhenny gained 82 yards in 14 tries, but 71 of those yards came on one carry.

## INSIDE THE FINISH

# What made the end so exciting:

 **ONCE UPON A TIME, THIS WAS TITLETOWN**
The Lions have won four NFL titles in their history. Here's how the four championship games went down:

 **1935; VS. NEW YORK**
In only their second year of existence, the Lions defeated the New York Giants, 26-7. Ace Gutowsky, Dutch Clark, Buddy Parker and Ernie Caddel each ran for scores.

 **1952; VS. CLEVELAND**
Bobby Layne and Doak Walker scored TDs and Pat Harder kicked a 36-yard field goal to help the Lions defeat Cleveland, 17-7.

DETROIT LIONS

Doak Walker catches a pass in the 1953 NFL title game. Walker scored a touchdown, and added a field goal and two extra points later in the game.

 **1953; VS. CLEVELAND**
Layne stymies Cleveland again, this time tossing a late touchdown pass to Jim Doran to win, 17-16.

 **1957; VS. CLEVELAND**
Backup Tobin Rote filled in for the injured Layne as the Lions routed the Browns, 59-14, for their last NFL championship of the 20th Century.

**THE DATE:** March 23, 1990

**THE LOCATION:** Superdome, New Orleans

**THE SETUP:**
One second left in a captivating Sweet 16 showdown. One phenomenal Georgia Tech freshman. One deep shot – after time expired – killed a dream and ended a magical Michigan State season. MSU fell victim to a ...

**THE ELEMENTS**

# Phantom buzzer-beater

### By MITCH ALBOM

It was after midnight when the glass slipper finally gave way.

One second. One miserable second. They were that far from another amazing victory, that far from sleeping on the doorstep of the Final Four. And then a freshman from New York City let fly a shot that would make any playground proud, and it fell through the nets and the miracle was on its way out.

Was it good? No. Is it over? Yes. That's what it comes down to. The replay of that final shot by Kenny Anderson that killed the Spartans' season clearly showed that it was released after the horn sounded.

But such is the nature of officiating and buzzer-beaters. There was plenty more basketball after that. An entire overtime period. Missed shots and missed opportunities that could have turned the scoreboard around. But the truth is, when Anderson's shot sliced through the nets, it sliced through the heart of the Spartan dream as well.

It went in? Yes. Was it good? No. But that didn't matter to Georgia Tech. The Yellow Jackets dived into a delirious pile on the floor, figuring it was a three-pointer and they had won. Even when told there were five minutes left, they carried that new life with them. And a dazed Spartan team, which had just about unlaced the gloves, had to string them up and keep fighting.

The magic was gone. Dwayne Stephens, who had hit two big free throws in the final minute of regulation, threw up an air ball from the baseline. Steve Smith, who had been brilliant all night, was stripped of the ball as he drove the lane. After Dennis Scott hit a leaner in the lane to put Tech ahead by one, the Spartans let four seconds run off the clock before calling time. And finally, Ken Redfield wound up with the ball, threw up a long prayer, and it clanged off the rim.

Georgia Tech 81, Michigan State 80.
End of season.
End of dream.

"It looked to me like when he released the ball, time was out," said disappointed Michigan State coach Jud Heathcote of Anderson's shot. "It was a great basketball game, and we have a great group of kids, but this was a tough loss for us."

The difference was Anderson. This kid is unbelievable. For most of the night, it was a showdown between him and Smith, one the playground legend from the Big Apple, the other

---

"It's not that teams don't play well against us.
We just play better defense than they're used to."

**JUD HEATHCOTE**, on the contrast between his defensive-minded team and Georgia Tech

"IT LOOKED TO ME LIKE WHEN HE RELEASED THE BALL, TIME WAS OUT."

**JUD HEATHCOTE**, on the game-tying shot by Georgia Tech's Kenny Anderson, later shown to come after the buzzer

DETROIT FREE PRESS

**PHANTOM BUZZER-BEATER: Freshman Yellow Jacket stings the Spartans**

DETROIT FREE PRESS

Michigan State's dream season, which included a Big Ten championship and a No. 1 seed in the NCAA tournament, ended in overtime against Georgia Tech.

> **"It was a great basketball game, and we have a great group of kids, but this was a tough loss for us."**
>
> **JUD HEATHCOTE,** on the loss in the NCAA Tournament to Georgia Tech

the lanky string bean from Detroit. Smith would worm inside people, bank in a jumper. Anderson would race down court, stop on a shadow, and bingo! Three points.

Smith would soar above people for a rebound, swiping those long arms, keeping the ball alive. Anderson would poke at Spartan guards like a stiletto, flicking the ball loose and streaking away like a thief.

He stole this one at (actually after) the buzzer.

Of course, the contrast between these teams was pretty sharp before they stepped on the court.

The Spartans came in defensive-minded, looking to shut down, close up, put a lid on the opponents.

"It's not that teams don't play well against us," Heathcote explained. "We just play better defense than they're used to."

Meanwhile, the Yellow Jackets never met a deficit they didn't like. Their last six victories were come-from-behind jobs, including a 17-point deficit that was erased against LSU. How do they do it? Anderson shoots. Brian Oliver shoots. Scott shoots. Their motto should be "Have guns, never tire."

And then there were the person-

alities. Heathcote, the old head-banger, runs a polite, disciplined, well-schooled program where everybody gets some spotlight but nobody walks around with a gold motto around his neck. Tech, by comparison, looks like the cast of "Saturday Night Live."

Led by the antics of blarney-stone Georgia Tech coach Bobby Cremins, a street-smart guy from the Bronx — the kind of coach who can swoop into New York City and come home with Anderson, the top high school player in the country in the 1988-89 season — the Jackets like to call themselves "Lethal Weapon 3." They clown around. They tease Cremins, they bust his chops.

Put it this way: John Salley went to Tech, played for Cremins, and was one of his favorite guys, shtick and all. Does that give you an idea?

About the only thing these teams had in common was winning — and the fact that people still couldn't believe they were doing it. The Spartans were picked for no better than fifth in most Big Ten previews, yet won the conference and attained a top-10 national ranking. Tech was supposed to be in a rebuilding year. Yet here were the Yellow Jackets, with a record of 26-6 and no defeats in March, and here were the Spartans, 28-5, who hadn't lost since Feb. 1.

Somebody would have to give.

It turned out to be the Spartans. They had intelligently weathered the Tech shooting threat. They had dominated the inside game, the major weak spot in the Georgia Tech arsenal. They had done everything they were supposed to do. They were just shot down. In the end, they were shot down by the amazing.

And so they go home, they walk off the Superdome floor dazed. And the tendency is to feel just awful.

Better to forget the final scene. Take these snapshots with you instead.

Matt Steigenga, the kid with the funny name, popping clean from the outside.

Kirk Manns, who looks like a well-scrubbed Bowery Boy, playing with that bum foot, burying a three-pointer.

Smith, who became hero-in-a-hurry, all long arms and legs and elbows, a basketball Gumby with a great shot.

Redfield, the senior, playing with the knowledge that any of these games could be his last as

DETROIT FREE PRESS

Georgia Tech's Kenny Anderson, middle, was part of the team's "Lethal Weapon 3" trio, along with Brian Oliver and Dennis Scott.

a Spartan, sacrificing what every kid wants, offense, to become a defensive force that in truth, enabled MSU to get this far. And Mike Peplowski, the personification of this blue-collar spirit, all thick muscle and crew cut and unbridled enthusiasm.

And orchestrating them all, Heathcote, Mr. Red In The

Face, doing it the way he's done it, hard, fair, clean. If you ever had a doubt about how good a coach this guy is, just consider what he did with this squad. What was it even doing here? All those injuries? All those supposedly better teams in the conference?

Better to remember them that way, happy, victorious. Sure,

they're home for good. Sure the season is over. Even so, no tears here. Only one team wins the whole thing. The others are graded by how hard they tried, how well they performed, and how much fun they brought to their fans and themselves.

High marks all around to the men in green. That was some kind of run.

NOT TILL THE FAT LADY SINGS **69**

**THE DATE:** March 21, 1986

**THE LOCATION:** Kemper Arena, Kansas City, Mo.

**THE SETUP:**
The Spartans were in command against No. 2 Kansas in Kansas City. Then time stopped for 15 seconds. The officials didn't adjust and the Jayhawks got new life. MSU never recovered, missing late free throws and allowing KU to prevail in ...

**THE ELEMENTS**

# The Great Clock-troversy

## By JACK SAYLOR

**U**nlike Superman, Lassie and John Wayne movies, the good guys don't always win.

So it was a clock malfunction, three missed foul shots in one-and-one situations and a very good Kansas basketball team that ended Michigan State's season-long revelry in overachievement.

Senior forward Calvin Thompson scored eight of his game-high 26 points in overtime, giving No. 2-rated Kansas a 96-86 victory over MSU before 16,800 fans.

The Spartans bowed out with a 23-8 record.

But the bizarre finish of regulation, which saw Kansas force overtime on Archie Marshall's tip-in with 10 seconds left, will leave the Spartans wondering what might have been for a long time.

MSU trailed, 46-37, at halftime with its outstanding guard combo of Scott Skiles and Darryl Johnson on the bench for seven minutes because of excess fouls.

"There were a lot of weird calls in the first half," MSU coach Jud Heathcote said. "We haven't had two guards on the bench with three fouls once all season."

But the Spartans, on the strength of some great second-half shooting, battled back and seemingly had gotten command with 2 1/2 minutes left.

Larry Polec scored after a rebound for a 75-72 lead, then Kansas lost its 6-foot-11 forward Danny Manning with his fifth personal with 2:21 left.

About then, the timer also lost control of the clock. It malfunctioned and play went on with no time expiring. Heathcote said about 10 seconds elapsed, but a CBS-TV clock indicated it was actually 15 seconds.

It proved costly to MSU, as Kansas pulled within two in that time frame.

"If the 10 seconds had gone off the clock, they wouldn't have had time to tie the score," Heathcote said. "What gets me is that I couldn't get the official to consult with the timer — they wouldn't even talk about it. There was no explanation. To have clock malfunction in the NCAA (tournament) is disappointing."

Kansas coach Larry Brown agreed.

"The thing that upset me is that they ignored it," he said. "There was 2:20 left — that is time for a lot of

> "What gets me is that I couldn't get the official to consult with the timer — they wouldn't even talk about it. There was no explanation. To have clock malfunction in the NCAA (tournament) is disappointing."
>
> **JUD HEATHCOTE**, on the disputed 15 seconds against Kansas in the 1986 NCAA tournament

"WE HAD OUR CHANCES.
WE MISSED THOSE
THREE FOUL SHOTS
DOWN THE END."

**JUD HEATHCOTE**, refusing to attribute complete blame for MSU's NCAA tournament loss to the officials

JULIAN H. GONZALEZ/DETROIT FREE PRESS

> "I've won several games for us this year and I take responsibility for this loss. If I'd made that free throw, the young freshman wouldn't have had to be there."
>
> **SCOTT SKILES**, on missing a late free thow in MSU's clock-aided loss to Kansas

things to happen so I'm not sure it made a difference."

Referee Bobby Dibler said that the clock malfunction was not a correctable error.

"It's got to be a scoring error to be a correctable error," Dibler said.

NCAA basketball committee chairman Dick Schultz made a postgame statement regarding clock operator Larry Bates.

"The clock operator was not aware the clock had malfunctioned, so he didn't notify the officials," Schultz said. "According to the rules, time cannot be added or subtracted from the clock unless the amount of time gained or lost is precisely known by the officials or the clock operator."

There was a second clock malfunction — this time with 19 seconds left. The clock continued to run after Kansas had fouled freshman Mark Brown, going down to one second while play was stopped.

The clock was reset the second time, restoring the 19 seconds.

Regardless, the Spartans still had a chance to lock up a victory. When Jayhawk Ron Kellogg fouled Skiles for his fifth personal with 1:49 left, coach Brown objected sufficiently to be called for a technical foul.

Skiles missed the front of his one-and-one, but made both the T's, giving MSU a 78-74 lead and possession of the ball.

Barry Fordham seemingly sealed it when he hit a jump shot — 80-74 and with only one minute left.

But Polec and Mark Brown missed the front of one-and-one situations after Jayhawk baskets and Marshall's tip tied the score with 10 seconds left.

"We had our chances," Heathcote said. "We missed those three foul shots down the end. We led the nation in free-throw percentage with more than 80%. Maybe it caught up with us."

Skiles, who rallied from two-man defensive pressure and first-half foul trouble to lead MSU with 20 points, tried to burden himself with

DAVID P. GILKEY/DETROIT FREE PRESS

Spartan legend Scott Skiles, showing off his jersey number during a ceremony in East Lansing in 1998, scored 20 points in MSU's tournament loss to Kansas.

blame for the loss.

"I've won several games for us this year and I take responsibility for this loss," he said. "If I'd made that free throw, the young freshman (Brown) wouldn't have had to be there."

After Marshall's basket, the Spartans declined to use their final timeout.

Instead, Skiles dribbled the length of the floor, then tossed up an off-balance 17-foot jumper that banged off the ring.

"I tried to get a better shot. Maybe I should have taken one more dribble and pulled up," said Skiles, who had seven assists. "But I didn't."

Heathcote passed on the timeout

since the ball was in Skiles' hands.

"With him in the open court, I felt we were better off, with Kansas not having time to set up a defense," he said.

The Spartans were in it only briefly in the extra session.

After Polec gave MSU an 84-82 lead, Kansas got a jumper from Cedric Hunter to tie it. Then Thompson's three-point play sent the Jayhawks on a roll — and the Spartans to the sideline.

Heathcote did not go out in good spirits, despite being very proud of his small but gritty ball club.

"I saw a lot of phantom fouls," Heathcote said. "I am very disappointed with the NCAA officials at this level."

# INSIDE THE FINISH

## What made the end so exciting:

### INSIDE THE CLOCK-TROVERSY

Details of the clock malfunction and the outcome of Michigan State's 96-86 loss to Kansas in the 1986 Sweet 16 matchup in Kansas City:

### FROZEN IN TIME

■ With 2:21 left in regulation, Kansas' Danny Manning commits his fifth foul. Vernon Carr misses the first free throw and sinks the second, increasing MSU's lead to 76-72.

■ Kansas' Greg Dreiling bounces an inbounds pass that Cedric Hunter, to save time, doesn't grab until the ball is near midcourt. One second ticks off the clock; the clock stops.

■ Hunter passes to Calvin Thompson on the wing. Thompson fires crosscourt to Ron Kellogg, who pitches back to Hunter at the top of the key. He drives the lane but misses a short jumper. Dreiling misses a tip. Kellogg scores on a putback, cutting the

MSU lead to 76-74. The clock shows 2:20 left — one second elapsed from Carr's free throws. It should have been 12 seconds, a computer scoring system used by the regional statistics crew confirmed. The computerized statistics, which include a clock that runs concurrently with the game clock, showed that the Kellogg basket came with 2:09 remaining.

■ MSU's Scott Skiles gets the inbounds pass. As he dribbles slowly toward midcourt, the clock finally starts, three seconds after Kellogg's basket. Replays revealed that 15 seconds had elapsed since the clock stopped.

### BICKERING COACHES

■ MSU coach Jud Heathcote rushes to the scorer's table to complain about the clock. The Kansas bench screams for a technical foul because Heathcote left his coaching box. The referees do not see Heathcote; no technical is called.

■ With the clock still running, MSU works the ball around the perimeter. When Skiles tries to dish off at the top of the lane, Kellogg is whistled for his fifth foul. The clock stops at 1:49. Kansas coach Larry Brown jumps off the bench to calm Kellogg. Heathcote yells at the referees — demanding that time be subtracted from the clock. Brown yells at the referees — arguing about Kellogg's foul and demanding that Heathcote be assessed a technical for leaving the coaching box. Brown is called for a technical (his program hit the referee's chest); no time comes off the clock.

### STATE'S LEAD BALLOONS

■ Skiles misses the front end of his one-and-one. The lead stays at 76-74. Skiles then hits two technical foul shots. MSU leads, 78-74.

■ The Spartans, without pressure from Kansas, pass around the perimeter to kill time. With

15 seconds left on the shot clock, they start looking for a good shot. Barry Fordham delivers, putting MSU ahead, 80-74 with 1:07 left.

### KANSAS RALLIES

■ Hunter rushes downcourt and hits a jumper with 58 seconds left. MSU leads, 80-76.

■ MSU goes into a spread offense, effectively passing around the perimeter. When Larry Polec drives the baseline, Chris Piper fouls Polec with 27 seconds left. The Spartans decide not to position anyone on the line for a possible rebound. Polec misses the front end of a one-and-one.

■ Archie Marshall rebounds and outlets to Hunter, who passes into the frontcourt to Thompson. He immediately drives the baseline and hits a 10-footer over Carr. MSU leads, 80-78, with 20 seconds left. Kansas calls its final time-out.

■ Skiles inbounds to Mark Brown in the backcourt and Mark Turgeon fouls immediately. The clock shows 19 seconds left. But the clock continues to run, going down to one second. Kansas coach Larry Brown approaches the scorer's table to demand more time. Heathcote yells: "What did you do the last time you didn't start it, huh?" The clock is restored to 19 seconds.

**Detroit Free Press**

**17**

THE DATE: February 20, 1998

THE LOCATION: White Ring, Nagano, Japan

THE SETUP:
Despite 15-year-old Tara Lipinski's wins in the U.S. and world championships in 1997, the '98 Olympics were supposed to belong to Michelle Kwan. Lipinski entered the long program trailing Kwan. But Lipinski delivered a finale of ...

THE ELEMENTS

# Pure gold

By JO-ANN BARNAS

She spun around in her sequined royal blue costume, bathed in a shower of white lights and flashbulbs that made Tara Lipinski glow like a full moon.

She was up there, top step, waving to the crowd, holding her Olympic gold medal in her tiny hands, saying to herself, "It's me. I can't believe it's me."

Tara Lipinski, the smallest Olympic champion, the youngest Olympic champion, the only Olympic champion with a collection of Beanie Babies, won Olympic gold by skating the performance of her young life.

"When I stepped onto the ice, I knew what the Olympics were all about — pure joy — and I put it into my program," said Lipinski, who trains at the Detroit Skating Club in Bloomfield Hills.

Lipinski, 15, did it all at White Ring. She won over six of the nine judges, who gave her 5.8s and 5.9s for artistic presentation — scores she hadn't seen all season.

She did it by landing all seven of her triple jumps, including her trademark triple loop-triple loop combination in front of the judges that she punctuated with a smile big enough to swallow the ice.

She did it by coming from behind, having finished second in the short program, second in all of her other events this season except one, since she won the world and U.S. championships in 1997.

But best of all for her, Lipinski did it by beating Michelle Kwan, the silver medalist, who seemed destined to be the gold-medal winner heading into the Winter Games. So lovely was Kwan's skating at U.S. nationals last month when she reclaimed her title from Lipinski that Kwan was compared to skating legends Janet Lynn and Peggy Fleming.

"For me, I felt like it was one of the best programs I had ever done, artistically and technically," said Kwan, 17. "I don't think I was perfect, but I skated my best."

All told, it was a wondrous night of skating at White Ring. And some say, because it featured the classic battle of No. 1 vs. No. 2, it also could be remembered as perhaps the biggest upset in Olympic figure skating history.

Never before had the runner-up U.S. champion beaten the defending U.S. titleholder in the Olympic

"When I stepped onto the ice, I knew what the Olympics were all about — pure joy — and I put it into my program."

TARA LIPINSKI, on her upset win in figure skating at the 1998 Nagano Games

"I FELT LIKE I COULDN'T DO ANYTHING WRONG OUT THERE. IT FELT SO GOOD AND SO PERFECT."

**TARA LIPINSKI**, on her gold medal-winning routine in Nagano

JULIAN H. GONZALEZ/DETROIT FREE PRESS

"She called me 10 minutes after she finished and said, 'Happy birthday, Dad.' Can you believe that?"

**JACK LIPINSKI,**
father of gold medalist Tara

JULIAN H. GONZALEZ/DETROIT FREE PRESS

Coach Frank Carroll consoles Michelle Kwan, who finished second to Tara Lipinski in the race for a figure skating gold medal.

Games.

Lipinski, who already was the youngest U.S. and world gold medalist at 14, shattered Sonja Henie's 70-year-old record by becoming the youngest Olympic gold medalist in an individual event. Henie, too, was 15 when she won her first of three gold medals in 1928, but Lipinski is younger by 60 days.

"There was something magical, special about this night," said Lipinski's mother, Pat. "When she left me this afternoon, she gave me a kiss and said, 'I'm going to do it.' And then she came back, knocked on the door, and said, 'Happy birthday, Mom.'"

JULIAN H. GONZALEZ/DETROIT FREE PRESS

The Detroit Skating Club's Tara Lipinski gets a congratulatory peck on the cheek during the medal ceremony from Michelle Kwan in the 1998 Nagano Games.

Pat Lipinski's birthday is Feb. 24, her father's is Feb. 28. Tara remembered that, too. When she left the kiss-and-cry area to do an interview with CBS, she borrowed a cellular phone and called her father.

"She called me 10 minutes after she finished and said, 'Happy birthday, Dad,' " Jack Lipinski said. "Can you believe that?"

The father then blew a deep breath and said, "I'm just so happy for her. At 15 years old, there is no way on God's green earth I could do something like that."

Asked what he thought when his daughter was finished with her long program, Jack Lipinski said, "After not breathing for 4 1/2 minutes, I thought, 'She went for it. She went for it like she told me she would.' "

The final group featured some of the best skating in years.

Kwan skated first, and she appeared as nervous for her performance as she was for her short program.

She seemed to skate deliberately, cautiously and slower than ever. Skating to "Lyra Angelica," she did seven triples but dragged a foot after her triple flip and received all 5.9s on the second mark for presentation. But she had left lots of room on her technical, receiving five 5.7s and the rest 5.8s.

"When I got off the ice, I wasn't thinking, 'Did I leave the door open?' " Kwan said. "I knew this competition wasn't a piece of cake. I was here looking for a good performance. I trained hard. It might not be the color medal I wanted, but I'll take it."

Lipinski had 20 minutes after Kwan's long program to get ready. She walked around nervously backstage and Richard Callaghan, her coach since December 1995, asked her to

remember the words she used to prepare herself for the Champions Series final in Munich, Germany, two months before the Olympics.

"I didn't want her to tell me what they were," Callaghan said. "I told her to use that same energy for this."

Lipinski did just that. Wearing silver sparkle eye shadow, she struck her pose and was off, her arms moving as wands, light as feathers.

She did everything great. Callaghan began smiling once she completed her double axel. When she landed her triple lutz-double toe loop right in front of the boards where he stood, Callaghan shouted, "That's gorgeous!"

Then came the camel combination spin, then footwork sequence. She was really feeling her music now. Skating to "The Rainbow" and "Scenes of Summer," Lipinski said she felt relaxed and happy on the ice.

And when it came time to attempt the triple flip — the same jump on which she fell in nationals — Lipinski didn't flinch. She threw herself into the air and came down lightly, another smile on her face.

The most important part for her, however, was still ahead — her sequence jump, the triple toe-half loop-triple salchow.

When she hung on to that, Callaghan banged his hands on the boards in delight once again.

And when she ended, she sprinted five steps before stopping and held her face in her hands, smiling so hard she nearly cried. Two days earlier, she had been good.

This night, she was better.

When her ordinals flashed on the scoreboard, showing her in first place, Lipinski jumped up and down and screamed, "I can't believe it!"

The Olympics had been an experience she had learned to

enjoy from beginning to end. While Kwan was sequestered in a hotel, Lipinski remained away from her parents and in the Olympic Village, where she has stayed since Feb. 5.

She had roommates and ate in the cafeteria like all the other athletes. She ate lunch with the U.S. women's hockey team. She stitched patches and made pillows in the sewing room and waited her turn to have her makeup applied at the Amway beauty counter.

"Just being in the village — that was the smartest thing we ever did," Pat Lipinski said. "She wanted the Olympic experience. She said, 'If I don't medal, at least I'll have that.' "

It was an unbelievable couple of weeks for Lipinski.

"I felt like I couldn't do anything wrong out there," Lipinski said. "It felt so good and so perfect."

**18**

THE DATE: October 27, 1979

THE LOCATION: Michigan Stadium, Ann Arbor

THE SETUP:
With the score tied, six seconds remaining and an unbeaten Big Ten season on the line against Indiana at home, the Wolverines had one chance. A tie was unacceptable, even with a backup QB and a freshman receiver. Michigan opted to ...

**THE ELEMENTS**

# Crank up the A.C.

BY MICK McCABE

**M**ichigan went to its spark plug — Anthony (A.C.) Carter — at precisely the right moment and pulled out a thrilling 27-21 victory over Indiana.

With the score tied and six seconds left, reserve quarterback John Wangler took the snap on Indiana's 45-yard line, dropped back and threw the ball 20 yards to Carter.

Carter caught the ball in the middle of the field, eluded two would-be tacklers at the 20 and outran one final defender into the end zone as time expired.

Carter was mobbed in the end zone and nearly crushed by his teammates as a sellout crowd of 104,832 at Michigan Stadium went berserk.

DETROIT FREE PRESS

Wide receiver Anthony Carter helped Michigan win two Big Ten titles between 1979 and 1982.

The touchdown capped a 78-yard drive that began with 51 seconds on the clock after Indiana had tied the game with 55 seconds left, refusing to try a two-point conversion to take the lead.

"I didn't think I had a chance to score," said Carter, the 5-foot-11, 155-pound freshman wide receiver. "A

guy made contact with me right away. Then a guy grabbed my left leg and I kind of lifted it up.

"The (second) guy almost got me down on the 2. But the game would have been over. After that, everybody crowded around me and I couldn't breathe."

After the touchdown, it was coach Bo Schembechler who was doing some heavy breathing as his team came away with the victory to keep the 10th-ranked Wolverines undefeated.

"It was a great play by Carter," Schembechler said. "I don't know of another man on our team who could have done that. As I saw him catch the ball, I thought he was going to stumble inside the 10.

"Our only hope was to go inside,

**"It was a great play by Carter. I don't know of another man on our team who could have done that. As I saw him catch the ball, I thought he was going to stumble inside the 10."**

BO SCHEMBECHLER, on freshman wide receiver Anthony Carter's game-winning touchdown against Indiana

Anthony Carter finished his career at Michigan with 161 catches, 37 touchdowns and 3,076 receiving yards.

DETROIT FREE PRESS

hoping we could get him between the free safety. Wangler did a great job of throwing it. You know we were going to get protection.

The escape by Carter, getting away from those guys, was the play. I didn't ever recall us winning on a

long play."

Wangler, who entered the game in the second quarter after B.J. Dickey suffered an injured shoulder, began the drive by hitting Butch Woolfolk for a seven-yard pass. On third down, Woolfolk gained two yards to set up a fourth-and-one. Schembechler went for the first down, and Woolfolk got it.

"My thinking was that we could have lost the game with that play and lost the Big Ten, too," Schembechler said.

"It could have been the biggest blunder of all time here. But I wanted to win this thing. We're going to pull out every stop to win the game."

Had U-M not picked up the first down, Indiana would have had the ball at about U-M's 31, in decent shape for a winning field goal.

On the next play, Wangler hit Ralph Clayton with a nine-yard gain with 25 seconds remaining. After an incompletion, Wangler threw a pass to fullback Lawrence Reid, who headed for the sideline after getting the first down and flipped the ball out of bounds with only six seconds left.

It was no fumble. Reid just tossed the ball out of bounds to stop the clock.

Indiana coach Lee Corso was livid, but Schembechler said it was perfectly legal.

"He fumbled the ball backward, so it was legal," said Schembechler. "If he wouldn't have done that, it would have cost us our last time-out. He saw he couldn't get to the sidelines, so he fumbled it out. If they would have fallen on it, it would have been their ball."

That gave U-M the ball at midfield. Before the Wolverines could get off another play, an Indiana lineman jumped offside, setting up U-M's winning play to Carter.

"We were looking for a miracle," Reid said. "And we got it."

**THE DATE:** November 9, 1974

**THE LOCATION:** Spartan Stadium, East Lansing

**THE SETUP:**

Woody Hayes might still be fuming about this one. Two rough halves weren't enough for MSU against the No. 1 Buckeyes. The Spartans were forced to wait 46 minutes until an official ruling was announced, but they got their ...

THE ELEMENTS

# Delayed gratification

### By CHARLIE VINCENT

GARY GARDINER/ASSOCIATED PRESS

Ohio State coach Woody Hayes wasn't in a smiling mood after MSU upset his top-ranked Buckeyes in a bizarre finish.

It was like a Cecil B. DeMille movie.

The cast of thousands sprawled in cinemascopic grandeur from one end of Spartan Stadium to the other, milling about aimlessly, or casually lounging in groups of two or three while the Michigan State band entertained during the 46-minute wait between the end of the MSU-Ohio State game and the official announcement of its outcome.

"The final score," a voice finally boomed over the public-address system, "Michigan State 16, Ohio State 13."

And what remained of the crowd of 78,533 broke into a thunderous cheer, then filed orderly out of the stadium for the delayed "happy hour."

It was Michigan State's biggest win in years, one deserving of the pande-monium caused by its many odd turns, topped by the indecision at the final gun that led to the long delay in making the Spartans' victory over the No. 1 team in the nation official.

Twice during the Buckeyes' final ill-fated drive, one of the officials over-ruled another, and the last mix-up came on the final play and caused Big Ten commissioner Wayne Duke — who watched the game from the press box — to go pale, then race to the officials' dressing room for an explanation.

Ohio State had marched 70 yards — to MSU's 1 — and appeared on the verge of snatching the victory away from Michigan State.

With 26 seconds left, Champ Henson smashed into the middle of the line.

Thud ... nothing. Nothing but a mass of green-shirted bodies lying on top of him and refusing to allow him

---

## "The final score ... Michigan State 16, Ohio State 13."

**PUBLIC ADDRESS ANNOUNCER,** 46 minutes after the end of the 1974 Michigan State-Ohio State game

MSU fullback Levi Jackson, a Detroit Kettering High grad, rumbles past Ohio State's defense for a stunning 88-yard touchdown in the fourth quarter. It proved to be the game-winner.

NOT TILL THE FAT LADY SINGS **81**

**The No. 1 team in the nation had to abandon its thunderous running game and resort to field goals — not once, not twice, but three times — as MSU stopped them at the 5, 3 and 8.**

to get off the ground and back into the OSU lineup.

Eventually, he made his way out of the tangle of arms and legs and took his place in the backfield. And the Buckeyes did run a play — a play that resulted in an official signaling "touchdown" and two others waving it off, indicating time had run out before the play was run.

Thousands of fans mobbed the field immediately while players and coaches from both teams tried to get an explanation of what had happened.

As Duke left the press box, he said: "Don't announce a thing until I return from the officials' dressing room."

So everybody hung by their fingernails for three quarters of an hour.

On the first play of that drive — which started with 3:11 remaining — Michigan State linebacker Terry McClowry came up with what, for a moment, appeared to be the game-saver.

He dived in front of a Cornelius Greene pass at OSU's 37-yard line. Head linesman Ed Scheck ruled it an interception, but umpire Frank Strocchia waved it off, contending McClowry dropped the ball.

It had been that kind of game from the start. A game of great individual efforts, mixed with bungled opportunities, hyperboles and contradictions.

Mike Hurd, one of the Spartans' most reliable receivers, was alone, with no one within 10 yards of him, when he dropped a Charlie Baggett pass on OSU's 20 during MSU's first possession.

He dropped another on the Buckeyes' 30 late in the first half, too. But he caught an 18-yarder from Baggett that put Hans Nielsen in position for a 39-yard field goal, allowing the Spartans to finish the first half tied at 3.

The Spartans allowed 19 first downs and 377 yards of total offense. But they frustrated the Buckeyes time and again inside the 10.

The No. 1 team in the nation had to abandon its thunderous running game and resort to field goals — not

ASSOCIATED PRESS

Buckeyes legend Archie Griffin rushed for 140 yards in the 1974 game against Michigan State. But few remember his performance, which was overshadowed by the controversial ending.

once, not twice, but three times — as MSU stopped them at the 5, 3 and 8. Tom Klaban kicked the first two, from 22 and 20 yards, but missed the third, leaving the Buckeyes with a 6-3 lead entering the fourth quarter.

A fumble by Baggett led to Ohio State's only touchdown with 5:57 left, and it appeared the Spartans' upset bid was doomed.

Steve Luke got the Buckeyes started, falling on Baggett's bobble at MSU's 44, and Henson ended the drive eight plays later by smashing in from the 1.

Then Michigan State struck with quickness and authority.

Baggett hit fullback Levi Jackson for 17 yards, Mike Jones for six, then found Jones alone behind safety Tim Fox and threw the 36-yard bomb that pulled the Spartans to within 13-9. Baggett passed to Jackson for the extra points, but the fullback fell short of the end zone.

But the Michigan State defense made the Buckeyes give the ball back four plays later. Ohio State's Tom Skladany punted all the way to the 12, and the Spartans found themselves 88 yards from the end zone.

And with the No. 1 team staring them in the face, few in the overflow crowd expected what would happen next.

Jackson, a 212-pounder from Detroit Kettering, slammed into the middle of the OSU line, found himself open, gave linebacker Arnold Jones a little fake, headed for the sideline and outran everybody as the crowd went wild and coach Woody Hayes went livid.

Nielsen converted, setting the stage for the fantastic finish.

And in all the excitement, no one even seemed to notice Archie Griffin gained 100 yards for the 19th straight game, rushing for 140.

## INSIDE THE FINISH
# What made the end so exciting:

### REPEAT PERFOMANCE: NOVEMBER 7, 1998, MSU REPRISED ITS GREAT UPSET OF OHIO STATE

The man whom skeptics denounced as devoid of emotion and incapable of motivating young men suddenly found himself sitting atop the college football world for one day.

The Spartans rallied from a 24-9 deficit in the third quarter and Renaldo Hill intercepted a Joe Germaine pass at the goal line with 1:12 left to seal the Spartans' 28-24 victory over the top-ranked Buckeyes.

But the moment following the upset was far from complete for Michigan State coach Nick Saban. He couldn't find the one person whose belief in his vision and principles never wavered.

"I've got to find Terry," Saban said, referring to his wife. "Where's Terry?"

An Ohio state trooper escorted Saban through a maze of media and delightfully stunned MSU athletic department officials to outside Ohio Stadium.

After hugging his mother, Mary Saban, he finally found Terry, tears streaming down her cheeks. Saban dropped his head on his wife's shoulder as they embraced.

TIMOTHY E. BLACK/ASSOCIATED PRESS

Michigan State quarterback Bill Burke helped dash Ohio State's hopes for a national championship in the Spartans' 28-24 upset in 1998.

"I had to keep looking at the final score on the scoreboard for a couple minutes because I just couldn't believe it," said receiver Gari Scott, one of many major contributors.

"We were already down by four touchdowns before we even took the field," sophomore receiver Plaxico Burress said of the point spread. "And then we wind up pulling off the biggest upset in the last few years against the No. 1 team in the nation."

Many will take away emotional souvenirs from one of the most special days in the history of Michigan State football.

Running back Sedrick Irvin's memento is a piece of turf from one of the Ohio Stadium end zones.

He's said he was going to put it in a little vase.

**By Drew Sharp**

MARK HALL/ASSOCIATED PRESS

OSU coach John Cooper was used to Michigan ruining his season, not Michigan State.

**20**

THE DATE: June 19, 1988

THE LOCATION: The Forum, Inglewood, Calif.

THE SETUP:

The Pistons were 60 seconds away from their first title. But the battle-hardened Lakers showed the Pistons weren't yet ready. Between Isiah Thomas' sprained ankle and letting the title slip away in the final seconds, the Pistons learned ...

**THE ELEMENTS**

# A painful lesson

### By CLIFTON BROWN

**N**ever have the Pistons given so much, played so well and fought so courageously, only to be so bitterly disappointed.

Detroit was 60 seconds away from winning its first NBA championship. But the Los Angeles Lakers never panicked, overcame a three-point deficit and won a classic playoff confrontation.

The Lakers' 103-102 victory in Game 6 at the Forum forced the deciding Game 7.

In the somber silence of the locker room afterward, it was hard for players to block out the pain.

"We were a minute away from winning it all," Pistons guard Joe Dumars said. "Considering that, yeah, I'd say this loss hurts more than any other."

Perhaps all of Detroit's emotions were mirrored on the postgame face of Isiah Thomas, who made a career playoff-high 43 points, eight assists and six steals. Thomas scored 25 points in the third quarter, an NBA Finals record for points in a quarter. His six steals tied an NBA Finals record held by three other players.

Thomas sat somberly in front of his locker with an ice bag on his swollen right ankle, which was sprained in the third quarter. His left little finger, which Thomas said might be dislocated, was injured in the first quarter.

X rays after the game were negative, though the ankle was severely sprained.

"We got a miraculous game from Isiah, as hurt as he was," Pistons coach Chuck Daly said. "He literally by himself got us back in the game. On offense, we didn't give him as much support as I would like.

"We were 45 seconds away from an NBA championship. What can I say?"

It came down to this — the Pistons leading, 102-99, with one minute left and the Lakers with the ball. After a Los Angeles time-out, Byron Scott nailed a 17-foot jumper with 52 seconds left, cutting Detroit's lead to one.

Detroit called time-out and set up a pick-and-roll play between Thomas and Bill Laimbeer.

"Billy had the shot," Daly said. "But he decided to pass to Zeke (Thomas), and then Zeke had to take a tougher shot."

Thomas missed an 18-footer over

---

**"We were a minute away from winning it all. Considering that, yeah, I'd say this loss hurts more than any other."**

**JOE DUMARS**, on the Pistons' last-minute loss to the Lakers in Game 6 of the NBA Finals

Trainer Mike Abdenour reacted quickly when Isiah Thomas fell to the floor in the third quarter. Thomas sored 25 points in that quarter.

# 20

> **"There was so much confu- sion."**
>
> **JOE DUMARS**, on his final shot, an off-balance bank shot with less than 10 seconds remaining

PAULINE LUBENS/DETROIT FREE PRESS

After losing Game 6 despite scoring 43 points, Isiah Thomas sat in a somber locker room, nursing his ankle.

PAULINE LUBENS/DETROIT FREE PRESS

Thomas was listed as doubtful for Game 7 with a severely sprained ankle, but he played in Detroit's defeat.

Michael Cooper. James Worthy rebounded, and the Lakers called time-out. Off the inbounds play, center Kareem Abdul-Jabbar attempted a 10-foot skyhook on the left base-line and missed, but Laimbeer was called for a foul. It was Laimbeer's sixth personal, removing him from the game.

Laimbeer refused to complain about the foul, saying, "It's part of the game."

And with 14 seconds left, Abdul-Jabbar made both free throws, giving the Lakers a 103-102 lead.

Detroit used its final time-out and called an option play for Thomas or Dumars to go one-on-one. But Thomas was knocked to the floor — colliding with teammate Adrian Dantley, who inbounded the ball — shortly after the inbounds pass. Dumars drove to the basket, ran into heavy traffic and threw up an off-balance bank shot. It missed.

Pistons forward Dennis Rodman momentarily got his hands on the ball, but it slipped away into Scott's hands. Rodman fouled Scott with five seconds left.

"There was so much confusion," Dumars said. "I just had to take off, drive to the hole and try to create something. There was a lot of traffic. There was small contact, but it wasn't enough to be called a foul."

Scott missed both free throws, but without any time-outs, Detroit never shot. John Salley fumbled the rebound off Scott's second miss, Thomas picked it up, then passed to Dantley at midcourt. The final buzzer sounded before Dantley could get off a desperation heave, and the Lakers ran jubilantly off the court.

So much will be remembered from this game. Thomas' surreal third quarter. Magic Johnson (22 points, 19 assists) playing with the spirit of a champion from start to finish. Worthy (28 points) flying to the basket as if swooping from the rafters.

Nonstop drama, with neither team leading by more than eight points.

"No one said it would be easy," Thomas said. "I'm not devastated. I want to win this championship. I'm willing to pay whatever it takes."

After Game 6, it was the Lakers were, too.

## INSIDE THE FINISH
## What made the end so exciting: A SAD CONCLUSION IN LOS ANGELES

PAULINE LUBENS/DETROIT FREE PRESS

Magic Johnson and Isiah Thomas were friendly rivals from the time Thomas entered the NBA in 1981. Game 7 was no laughing matter.

INGLEWOOD, Calif. — Hobbled and bruised, courageous but playing against a team bent on taking its place in history, the Pistons fell short in their quest for an NBA championship.

The Los Angeles Lakers won their second straight NBA title, defeating Detroit, 108-105. And the Lakers did it the hard way, overcoming a 3-2 deficit in the series by winning Games 6 and 7 at the Forum.

Lakers forward James Worthy, who had a triple-double with 36 points, 16 rebounds and 10 assists, was named the most valuable player of the series.

"To win a championship, you've got to be damn good, but you've also got to be damn lucky," said Isiah Thomas, who scored 10 points and played 28 valiant minutes on a severely sprained right ankle.

Detroit trailed by 15 points early in the fourth quarter, came back strong, but fell short. With the Pistons trailing, 103-100, with a minute left, Bill Laimbeer missed a jumper and after a scramble for the rebound, the Pistons lost the ball out of bounds.

John Salley blocked Worthy's shot on the next possession, but on the trip downcourt, Dennis Rodman missed a 14-foot jumper. Byron Scott rebounded and was fouled with 30 seconds left. Scott nailed both free throws, giving the Lakers a 105-100 lead with 30 seconds left. On Detroit's next possession, Laimbeer threw a bad pass to Joe Dumars and Magic Johnson stole it. Michael Cooper was fouled immediately, missed both free throws, and Dumars made a lay-up to make it 105-102 with 16 seconds left.

Worthy was fouled with 14 seconds left, missed the first free throw, but made the second. Laimbeer hit a three-pointer to make it 106-105 with six second left. But on the inbounds pass, Magic Johnson hit A.C. Green with a long pass for a breakaway lay-up with two seconds left. Detroit inbounded to Thomas at midcourt, but he fell to the floor without getting a shot.

"This is pretty hard to take," said Adrian Dantley, who scored 16 points but sat out the final 10:22.

"Game 6 was the game we should've won. We had them, but we didn't put them away."
**By Clifton Brown**

# Third team

 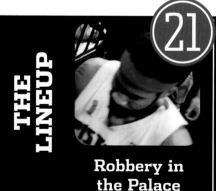

**THE ELEMENTS**
Look for these eight elements in each of the 50 thrilling finishes:

**THE BIG COLLAPSE**

**THE BIG COMEBACK**

**CONTROVERSY STRIKES**

**THE HEART-BREAKER**

**HIGH STAKES**

**INDIVIDUAL EFFORT**

**VS**

**THE BIG RIVALRY**

**TEAM EFFORT**

"These are the moments you've got to savor, man."

**KIRK GIBSON**, on blowing kisses to the fans in Tiger Stadium after his second home run in Game 5 of the 1984 World Series practically guaranteed a title for the Tigers

**26** Special delivery

**27** Hail, yes!

**28** Championship connection

**29** Poor decision, rich reward

**30** A kick went amiss

**21**

**THE SETUP:**

The Palace was rocking. The Pistons' faithful were expecting to take a 3-2 lead in the NBA Finals against the San Antonio Spurs. But Rasheed Wallace left Robert Horry open and he nailed the winning triple, prompting Pistons fans to yell ...

**THE ELEMENTS**

# Robbery in the Palace

DAVID P. GILKEY/DETROIT FREE PRESS

### By MITCH ALBOM

**Y**ou don't leave him alone. You never leave him alone. But there he was, alone, at his favorite killer spot, the three-point line, Rasheed Wallace had gotten snookered, and by the time Tayshaun Prince went charging toward the killer, like a man trying to save a dog from a speeding bus, it was too late. The killer lined it up. The killer got it in his sights. The killer fired.

The killer hit.

The Pistons were like a classic album in a wonderful groove and then someone stomped on the ground and the needle jumped. Groove over. Scratch heard. Their streak of home victories in the NBA Finals ended in overtime, just after midnight, broken up by a 34-year-old bench player who seems to do this to somebody every year. Game 5 was the Pistons' turn to have their music interrupted by Robert Horry.

Horry-fied.

**"I was shooting pretty good, so I was gonna let it fly."**

**ROBERT HORRY**, on taking the last-second shot that beat the Pistons in Game 5 of the 2005 NBA Finals

"YOU TALK ALL YEAR
ABOUT THE THINGS
YOU WANT TO ACCOMPLISH ...
IF EVERYBODY GETS IT,
YOU DON'T GET IN THAT SITUATION."

**LARRY BROWN**, Pistons coach, defending Rasheed Wallace, above, after his defensive mistake in Game 5

REGINA H. BOONE/DETROIT FREE PRESS

NOT TILL THE FAT LADY SINGS **91**

# 21

"Actually, I wasn't even thinking about a three-pointer. It was supposed to be a pick-and-roll with Tim (Duncan) and I saw Rasheed bite and I said, 'Oh, let me stay out here.' "

**ROBERT HORRY**, on taking advantage of Rasheed Wallace's mistake on defense to get open for a game-winning three-pointer

JULIAN H. GONZALEZ/DETROIT FREE PRESS

Robert Horry jams one home as the Pistons' Ben Wallace and the Spurs' Tim Duncan look on. Horry saved his best bucket for last.

"I was shooting pretty good," Horry told ABC after the game was over and the Palace was deflated and the Spurs had prevailed in overtime, 96-95, thanks to his three-point miracle, "so I was gonna let it fly."

Let it fly. And let it die. They call him Big-shot Bob, and you didn't need any more evidence than this game to see why. Horry's dagger had blood all over it. He hit one three-pointer. He hit another. He hit a huge slam in overtime and got fouled. He had no points in the first half, three in the third quarter and 18 the rest of the way, including hitting five out of six three-pointers.

If there is one thing you don't allow to happen against any team with Robert Horry on it, it's giving him the chance to make a big shot. He has been doing it his whole career. He has done it for the Houston Rockets. He has done it for the Los Angeles Lakers. He has done it for the Spurs.

Rasheed Wallace committed a space cadet move, doubling the wrong guy, Manu Ginobili, leaving Horry alone. You can't fault one guy for a loss. But you can fault one guy for a play that leads to one.

Horry-fied.

"I guess there was a miscommunication," Pistons coach Larry Brown said, trying to protect Wallace. "You talk all year about the things you want to accomplish ... if everybody gets it, you don't get in that situation. If everybody doesn't ... it ultimately falls on me."

No it doesn't. Brown doesn't wear shorts, and he doesn't play. The Pistons are smart enough to know better. Rasheed is smart enough to know better. The ball went into Ginobili. A two-point basket would have only tied the score. They could live with that. Only

ERIC SEALS/DETROIT FREE PRESS

Rasheed Wallace and the Pistons recovered from the Game 5 heartbreaker in Game 6, but Tim Duncan led the Spurs to the title in the finale.

one thing was forbidden — a three-point basket.

And that's what they allowed.

"Actually, I wasn't even thinking about a three-pointer," Horry said. "It was supposed to be a pick-and-roll with Tim (Duncan) and I saw Rasheed bite and I said, 'Oh, let me stay out here.'

"Since I was shooting well, I wanted to let it fly. I'm the type of player I want to win a game. ... I'm always going to go for a three."

Horry-fied.

No blowout this time

Overtime it was. It was traded baskets. It was traded steals. It was traded blocks, traded fouls, traded spots atop the scoreboard. Not to put too much of a cliché on it, but you did find yourself saying "Who wants it more?" and you came up with a different answer every 24 seconds.

It was Ginobili coming back to life, Tony Parker exploding in the first half, and Duncan (26 points) playing the part of the android that won't quit (except at the free-throw line and except at the very end, when he tightened up). And it was Chauncey Billups pulling up for jumpers and Antonio McDyess hitting the boards hard and Prince elevating for one-handed floaters that defied natural law.

But in the end it was Horry, with his momentum-killing three-pointers, seven rebounds and some smart playmaking. He pulled a victory out of defeated air. The Pistons should have been up, three games to two. Instead, they faced a Herculean task.

"That's Big-shot Bob!" Duncan gushed after the victory. "He does whatever he wants to do."

Well, he seems to when a big game is on the line.

The Pistons know that. They just didn't get him covered. That's what the Pistons do, get people covered. They didn't this time. It's that simple.

**22**

THE DATE: October 30, 2004

THE LOCATION: Michigan Stadium, Ann Arbor

THE SETUP:
The Spartans had a 17-point lead in the fourth quarter at the Big House.
U-M quarterback Chad Henne decided to look for his No. 1 target, who wore
that jersey number. At the end of this thriller, MSU learned that ...

THE ELEMENTS

# Overtime means Braylon time

By JOHN ELIGON AND JEMELE HILL

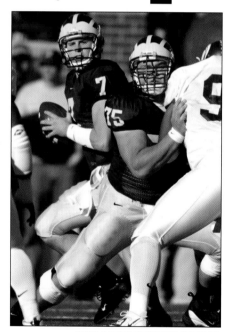

JULIAN H. GONZALEZ/DETROIT FREE PRESS
Michigan quarterback Chad Henne (7) rebounded
from a tough first half against Michigan State
to finish with 273 yards.

**M**ichigan State often complains that Michigan doesn't respect the rivalry — especially when the games are played in Ann Arbor.

Well, the Spartans finally might have won the Wolverines' respect. But MSU still hadn't won a game at Michigan Stadium since 1990.

MSU outplayed U-M for 3 1/2 quarters before the Wolverines scored 17 unanswered points late in the fourth and won, 45-37, in triple overtime.

It was the Wolverines' third straight victory over the Spartans and their seventh in a row at home.

In the third overtime, Michigan quarterback Chad Henne hit Braylon Edwards on a crossing pattern on third-and-nine, and the senior took it 24 yards for a touchdown. Henne completed a pass to tight end Tim Massquoi for the two-point conversion and the final score.

The Spartans had a chance to answer, but quarterback Damon Dowdell's pass on fourth down flew over the head of wideout Aaron Alexander.

"You got to love it when you're on the edge," said U-M linebacker LaMarr Woodley. "We were on the edge and we came out here and we won. It's real nice to beat Michigan State. They came in here, they were talking and they didn't back it up."

For most of the game, the Spartans did back it up. The Spartans' ground game absolutely shredded the Wolverines, piling up 368 yards on the nation's No. 3 rush defense.

Tailback DeAndra Cobb finished with a career-high 205 yards, and he

"You got to love it when you're on the edge. We were on the edge and we came out here and we won. It's real nice to beat Michigan State. "
LaMARR WOODLEY, on beating Michigan State in three overtimes in 2004

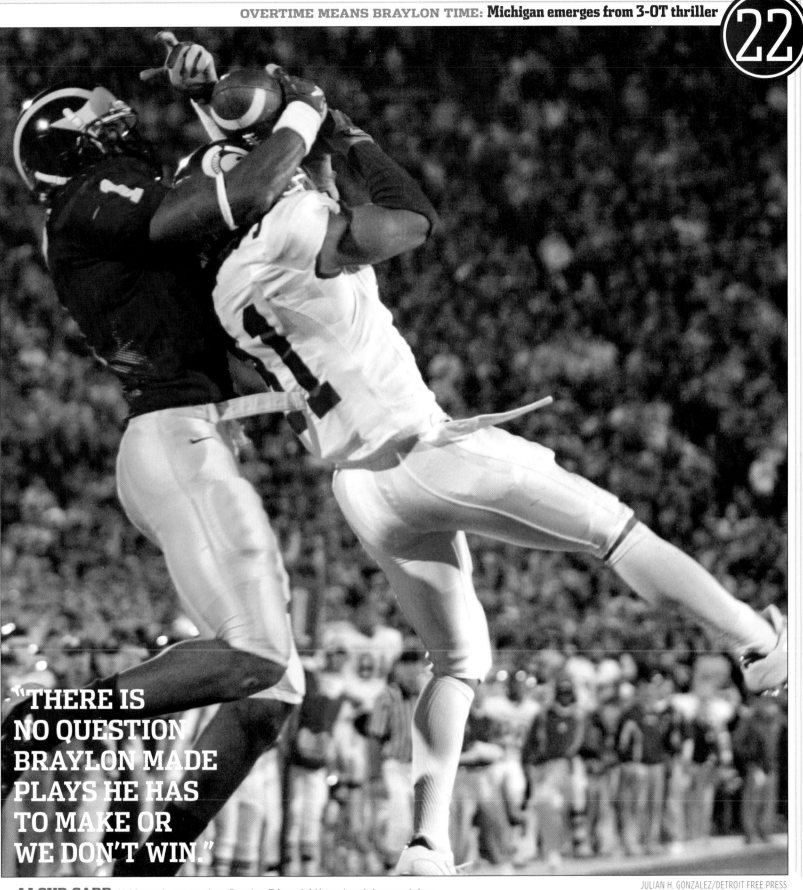

"THERE IS
NO QUESTION
BRAYLON MADE
PLAYS HE HAS
TO MAKE OR
WE DON'T WIN."

**LLOYD CARR**, U-M coach, on receiver Braylon Edwards' three touchdown catches

JULIAN H. GONZALEZ/DETROIT FREE PRESS

"They won it, and we didn't make the plays to win it. We played a good football team and we played well, at times."

**JOHN L. SMITH**, MSU coach, on his team's effort against Michigan in a triple-overtime thriller

JULIAN H. GONZALEZ/DETROIT FREE PRESS

Freshman tailback Mike Hart had 33 carries for 224 yards and scored a touchdown in Michigan's triple-overtime victory against Michigan State.

slid through U-M's defense for lengthy touchdown runs of 72 and 64 yards.

"They won it, and we didn't make the plays to win it," said coach John L. Smith. "We played a good football team and we played well, at times.

We made some mistakes, but for the most part, we controlled the football game. When it came time to win it at the end, they had a lot of momentum going there and they made some big-time plays."

After Cobb's 64-yard score on a

draw play, the Spartans were ahead, 27-10, and just 8:43 separated them from one of their most dominating wins ever over U-M.

But the Wolverines erased that possibility in a span of 3:46. U-M kicker Garrett Rivas reduced MSU's lead to

27-13 with a 24-yard field goal with 6:27 left in regulation.

After Rivas' score, Brian Thompson recovered a Troy Nienberg onside kick. U-M went to its playmakers, tailback Mike Hart and Edwards. After the onside kick, Hart — whose 224 rushing yards against MSU marked his third consecutive 200-yard game — caught a screen pass for 11 yards and got an extra 15 tacked on when linebacker David Herron grabbed his face mask. That set up a 36-yard touchdown pass from Henne to Edwards, who leaped over 5-foot-9 cornerback Jaren Hayes and ripped the ball from his hands, making the score 27-20 with 6:12 remaining.

Three minutes after his first TD, Edwards outleapt Hayes again for a 21-yard score, tying the game at 27. Edwards scored three of the Wolverines' last four TDs, part of an 11-catch, 189-yard day that cemented him in U-M's record books. The three TDs were a career best, and the yardage allowed him to surpass receiver Anthony Carter as the school's all-time receiving yards leader.

"There is no question Braylon made plays he has to make or we don't win," U-M coach Lloyd Carr said. "Those were great catches. All three of those catches were plays where the defender was in pretty good position."

The performance of the U-M offense in the latter part of the game was a stark contrast to what it had done the rest of the

JULIAN H. GONZALEZ/DETROIT FREE PRESS

Michigan wide receiver Jason Avant scored a touchdown in the second OT on a five-yard pass from Chad Henne.

game.

In the first half, Henne completed only 8-for-15 for 56 yards. Edwards was held to three catches for 35 yards. And MSU's defense, which had the fewest sacks in the Big Ten, got to Henne three times in the first half and four overall. But Henne rebounded, passing for 273 yards and four scores after

completing 24-for-35.

While U-M celebrated one of its greatest victories, the Spartans were dealt one of their most devastating losses — and not just because of the final score.

Quarterback Drew Stanton, who kept the U-M defense off-balance, left the game in the second quarter with a separated

right shoulder. Before he was knocked out of the game, he gained 80 yards on the ground — including a five-yard touchdown run — and 95 in the air.

"We fought to the end, and it's no doubt we should have won that game," linebacker Ronald Stanley. "We just came up short, but I think we earned a lot of respect ... "

**"We fought to the end, and it's no doubt we should have won that game. We just came up short, but I think we earned a lot of respect ..."**

**RONALD STANLEY**, Michigan State linebacker, on what he and his teammates took away from their triple-overtime loss to Michigan

THE DATE: November 19, 1966

THE LOCATION: Spartan Stadium, East Lansing

THE SETUP:
The 'Game of the Century' featured the storied Notre Dame Fighting Irish, the No. 1 team in the nation, vs. Duffy Daugherty's scrappy Michigan State squad, right behind them at No. 2. Each entered the game undefeated. They finished ...

THE ELEMENTS

# On equal footing

BY JACK BERRY AND HAL McCOY

Duffy Daugherty wouldn't say it, but his Michigan State players did.

"As far as I'm concerned," said co-captain Clint Jones, "we're No. 1. We played like champions.

"When we were in our territory and had fourth down, we gambled. We played to win and that's the only way to play the game. They played to tie.

"They've got a good team but I won't say that a team that eats up the clock is a great team."

The 10-10 "Game of the Century" left a bittersweet taste in everyone's mouth. There was mumbling in the stands by fans from both schools, loud boos as Notre Dame killed the clock in the final minute instead of trying to pass.

"I thought they'd try to throw a

MICHIGAN STATE UNIVERSITY
MSU and Notre Dame played to a tie, the most famous one in college football history.

long bomb, at least on that last play," said defensive star George Webster.

It was sentiment repeated throughout the Spartans' dressing room.

"We were going for broke," Daugherty said, "not that ties aren't better than losing — they are."

Daugherty showed how much he wanted this game with a courageous

call on State's final possession.

With fourth and a foot at MSU's 29, 3:35 left in the game, Daugherty ordered his team to go for the first down.

Notre Dame linebacker Pete Duranko grabbed quarterback Jimmy Raye behind the line of scrimmage, but Raye wiggled across the 30.

It was for naught. Three plays later, Dick Kenney punted from the 36 and Notre Dame ran out the clock.

Daugherty wouldn't let himself get pinned into saying he was surprised that Notre Dame didn't pass at the end.

"We just kept calling time-outs, hoping we could get the ball back for a field goal try," he said.

Michigan State struck out to a 10-0 lead in the first half on a four-yard

"When we were in our territory and had fourth down, we gambled. We played to win and that's the only way to play the game. They played to tie."

CLINT JONES, Michigan State co-captain, on the Spartans' 10-10 tie with Notre Dame that left both teams undefeated

MICHIGAN STATE UNIVERSITY

MSU fans booed Notre Dame's tactics in the closing moments of the game. At the end of the season, the Irish finished No. 1 in the AP and UPI polls.

> "We were going for broke. Not that ties aren't better than losing — they are."
>
> **DUFFY DAUGHERTY**, MSU coach on his game plan in the fourth quarter

smack by Reggie Cavender and a 47-yard field goal by Kenney.

Notre Dame shortly chopped it to 10-7 on a 34-yard pass from Coley O'Brien to Bob Gladieux, and tied the score on the first play of the final period on a 28-yard field goal by Joe Azzaro.

Azzaro had a chance to win it with four minutes left, but his 41-yard try was long enough, leaving the huge throng breathless until the kick was signaled wide to the right.

How about No. 1 now?

"I think both teams are worthy of it," Daugherty said. "I don't think it's ever been done, but I don't think there ever was a situation like this where both clubs had unblemished records and met at the end of the season."

Notre Dame athletic director Moose Krause pushed into the crowded equipment room where Duffy met the media and congratulated Daugherty.

"I just told them we should be co-champs," Daugherty said.

"I'll go for that and I've got a vote," Krause said.

Threading through

Daugherty's postmortem was the phrase "field position."

"For the last two quarters we were getting the ball inside our 5-yard line and it's pretty tough to do something from there," Daugherty said. "It was just about the kind of football game everybody thought it would be."

Except that no one thought Notre Dame would fall on the ball.

"I'd have liked to have played another half," Webster said.

And the Spartans taunted the Irish over the line in

those dying seconds when State twice called time-out, trying to get the ball back.

"C'mon, sissy," big Bubba Smith yelled.

Bubba admitted the Irish did some talking, too.

"That left tackle, No. 71 (Paul Seiler), got a thrill out of running off his mouth. But he's a good boy."

And that's the way it ended — grudging respect for the physical capabilities of the Irish, but great disappointment with the tie and the fact that Notre Dame went for the tie.

**THE DATE:** November 24, 1973

**THE LOCATION:** Michigan Stadium, Ann Arbor

**THE SETUP:**
It was supposed to settle the Big Ten, a Rose Bowl berth and a possible national title, but after a hard-fought battle ended tied, U-M and OSU were forced to put Pasadena hopes on hold for one more day, as everyone wondered ...

# California, here *who* comes?

**By CURT SYLVESTER**

**W**ith an utter disregard for the tradition, the legend and the general mayhem of this rivalry, mighty Michigan and awesome Ohio State performed the unthinkable.

The Wolverines and Buckeyes battled to a 10-10 standoff before a Michigan Stadium record crowd of 105,223 in a game that was intended to decide the Big Ten title, a possible national championship and the Rose Bowl berth.

What it did, on a damp and dreary day, was give U-M and OSU an equal share of the conference title, jar the Buckeyes from any national championship hopes and leave the bowl bid hanging until the following day, when the Big Ten's athletic directors were scheduled to vote on which team to send to Pasadena.

The Wolverines lost star quarterback Dennis Franklin with a broken collarbone late in the fourth quarter after he had brought them from a 10-0 halftime deficit to the tie.

The Wolverines finished 10-0-1, the Bucks 9-0-1. In the Big Ten, they were 7-0-1.

And whom do you blame for the tie?

Coach Woody Hayes, docile on the sideline all afternoon, had second-string quarterback Greg Hare (the best of OSU's passers) throwing from deep in his own territory the last four times he had the ball.

And U-M coach Bo Schembechler had ace kicker Mike Lantry booming away from 38 and 44 yards out in two desperation field-goal tries.

"I'm really disappointed in the tie," Schembechler said after spending about 15 minutes with his players. "But I'm extremely proud of the way our players came back. That took a lot of character and a lot of pride.

"I'll tell you this. We didn't settle for a tie. We would have done anything to win this game."

The two halves of the contest could have been two entirely different games.

The Buckeyes, moving on the legs of unstoppable tailback Archie Griffin, controlled the first half; the Wolverines, perked up by fullback Ed Shuttlesworth's powerful inside running, dominated in the second half.

If the Bucks had the look of No. 1 in the first half, the Wolverines had it in the second.

The Bucks got a 31-yard field goal from Blair Conway and a five-yard touchdown run by freshman fullback Pete Johnson in the first half.

The Wolverines got a 30-yard field goal from Lantry and a 10-yard touchdown run by Franklin in the second half.

And tradition be damned, neither

---

**"We didn't settle for a tie. We would have done anything to win this game."**
**BO SCHEMBECHLER**, Michigan coach, on having kicker Mike Lantry attempt two long field goals late in the game

### THE BITTER END

A shocked and angry Bo Schembechler lashed out at Big Ten officials and athletic directors for denying his unbeaten Michigan team the opportunity to play in the Rose Bowl, instead voting to send the Ohio State Buckeyes. "There's no question about it, I'm very bitter," snapped the coach after learning Ohio State had been selected as the Big Ten representative. "I resent it. It's a tragic thing for Big Ten football." Athletic directors were polled by phone through the Big Ten office in Chicago. Commissioner Wayne Duke called U-M athletic director Don Canham with their decision.

"I couldn't believe it," Canham said. "It's just unbelievable." He had predicted U-M would be picked, possibly 9-1. MSU athletic director Burt Smith told the Free Press that Dennis Franklin's broken collarbone, suffered in the fourth quarter of the 10-10 tie with Ohio State, might have had an effect on the athletic directors' decisions. There was little doubt in Schembechler's mind, however, that the injury to his first-string quarterback threw the vote to OSU.

"There was petty jealousies involved, and they used the injury to Dennis Franklin as a scapegoat."

How they voted, according to the Free Press' poll days after the game:

For Michigan: Iowa, Minnesota, Michigan.

For Ohio State: Illinois, Indiana, Michigan State, Northwestern, Ohio State and Purdue.

Wisconsin's pick was unknown.

**By Curt Sylvester**

ASSOCIATED PRESS

U-M's Bo Schembechler went 5-4-1 against Ohio State coach Woody Hayes. That tie, in 1973, was one of the most controversial games in the series. It didn't get better the following season for Schembechler, as U-M lost, 12-10. And in that game, Michigan kicker Mike Lantry missed a last-second field goal.

team was about to give up another touchdown, field goal or safety the rest of the afternoon. A tie it was to be.

To come from a 10-0 half-time deficit, Michigan's defense had to hold Griffin to 64 second-half yards (after 99 in a devastating opening half) and limited elusive quarterback Cornelius Greene to 20 yards (after 12 in the first half).

The rest depended on Franklin's execution, his occasional passes to wingback Clint Haslerig or tight end Paul Seal, and Shuttlesworth running behind the blocking of his front five — center Dennis Franks, guards Mike Hoban and Dave Metz and tackles Jim Coode and Curtis Tucker.

The Wolverines showed their intentions from the moment they took the second-half kickoff, driving from their 28 to the OSU 32

before a Franklin toss into the end zone was picked off by defensive back Neal Colzie.

But the Bucks weren't going anywhere against U-M, led by linebackers Carl Russ and Steve Strinko, and safety Dave Brown.

When U-M stopped Greene on a fourth-and-two at the Michigan 43, Franklin got them moving again.

Haslerig caught an 11-yard pass for a first down, Shuttlesworth knocked off 11 yards in two carries and then 12 in two more. That's the way it went. Shuttlesworth carried time and again until the Buckeyes halted the drive at their own 13, forcing Lantry's field goal from the 20.

After a short OSU punt moments later, U-M had it at midfield. A 35-yarder from Franklin to Seal got Michigan within range.

And on fourth down and inches at the 10, Franklin

faked to the big fullback at the middle, then cut neatly inside the defensive end to score the touchdown.

The Wolverines were moving again late in the game from their 11 to the Ohio State 49, with Franklin passing a pair of 14-yarders to Haslerig and a seven-yarder to Shuttlesworth.

Then it happened. Franklin was hit as he threw, landing hard on his right shoulder and suffering a broken collarbone.

After two plays behind second-string quarterback Larry Cipa, the U-M faced a fourth-and-two situation.

Lantry tried a 48-yard field goal; it had the distance but ended less than 24 inches to the left of the upright.

Ohio State's first pass was intercepted by U-M defensive back Tom Drake at the OSU 33. Moments later, with less than 30 seconds left, Lantry's field-goal try went wide to the right.

**25**

**THE SETUP:**
Even before the resilient Tigers beat the St. Louis Cardinals in the 1968 World Series, there were plenty of memorable moments. None was more special than the rally that put Denny McLain on a lofty pedestal. His 30th win meant that ...

**THE ELEMENTS**

# Dizzy loves company

BY **GEORGE CANTOR** AND **JACK SAYLOR**

The Tigers won Denny McLain his 30th game and sent goose pimples down the back of the entire country.

Roaring from behind in the ninth inning, just like it has done all season, Detroit pulled it out for McLain in a win-it-or-bust rally, 5-4.

The victory made McLain the first pitcher to win 30 games since 1934. The whole country, and 44,087 fans at Tiger Stadium, watched the drama unfold in spellbound fascination.

Willie Horton capped the two-run comeback by belting a drive just beyond the reach of Oakland's pulled-in leftfielder, Jim Gosger, to knock in Mickey Stanley and touch off the wildest scene at Tiger Stadium in 30 years.

Detroit had to pull it out in the ninth because McLain was removed for a pinch-hitter in the inning. If the team had merely tied the game, the decision would have been in the hands of another pitcher, and Denny would have had to wait.

But as Stanley danced across the plate, the Tigers exploded from the dugout, led by McLain. First they mobbed Stanley, then the entire team rushed to grab Horton. Stanley finally picked up McLain and hauled him off the field.

But the fans wouldn't go home. They stood at their seats yelling for McLain until the pitcher came back onto the field to take a bow.

Even then, several hundred fans stayed outside the Tigers clubhouse, chanting, "We want Denny!" long after the players had gone.

McLain wrote a new page of baseball history, and nobody was any happier about it than Jerome Herman Dean, a similar author.

Ol' Diz threw his arms around McLain amid the wild scene after the Tiger wonderboy had joined Dean in the 30-game winner's circle and offered his congratulations.

"I got a great thrill out of it," the old Cardinal superstar shouted to Denny. "And to win it in the ninth inning like that ... it's one of the greatest games I ever saw."

McLain was almost too overcome with excitement to reply.

"Thank you, thank you, thank you," he repeated. "This is the greatest team I could ever play for — the way they came from behind to win it for me."

---

**"I got a great thrill out of it. And to win it in the ninth inning like that ... it's one of the greatest games I ever saw."**

**DIZZY DEAN**, congratulating Denny McLain on his 30th win of the season; Dean was the last pitcher to win as many, doing so in 1934

DETROIT FREE PRESS

Denny McLain's teammates weren't the only ones to offer their congrats after he won his 30th game of the 1968 season. Dizzy Dean gave McLain a hug, too.

> "This is the greatest team I could ever play for — the way they came from behind to win it for me."
>
> **DENNY McLAIN**, Tigers pitcher, on winning his 30th game thanks to a bottom-of-the-ninth rally by the Tigers

McLain stuck the prized game-winning ball in the top of his locker. It will join the other 29 "winners" on the mantel at his home.

Reggie Jackson, the young Oakland rightfielder, looked as though he was going to steal the spotlight. He belted two home runs, cut down one runner at the plate and made a leaping catch to account for the 4-3 score as the Tigers came up in the ninth.

Diego Segui, who had entered the game in the fifth, had choked off Detroit on three singles. The only runs scored on a three-run Norm Cash

homer in the fourth that had given Detroit a brief lead.

But Al Kaline batted for McLain to start the ninth inning and worked Segui for a walk.

Dick McAuliffe fouled off two sacrifice bunts and finally fouled to third baseman Sal Bando in front of the silent Detroit dugout.

But Stanley ripped a solid single right over second base as Kaline, showing no trace of his leg injury, darted around to third.

The next hitter was Jim Northrup. He tapped a slow roller down the first-base line, and in the game's

biggest play, Kaline broke for the plate.

Danny Cater raced in for the ball and made an off-balance throw that sailed over the head of catcher Dave Duncan. Kaline and Duncan collided, with Kaline scrambling for the plate on his hands and knees to score as Stanley galloped to third.

Horton came up and Segui took him to a 2-2 count. All the Oakland players were drawn in close for a play at the plate.

Horton hit one that Gosger would have caught if he had been playing at normal depth — but

Stanley would have scored anyhow after the catch.

Horton was given a single on the hit — which was the most ignored scoring decision of the year.

McLain wound up giving up six hits, walking just one and striking out 10.

McLain said this wasn't the toughest game he'd ever pitched.

"It just seemed like the toughest," he said.

And how about a victory celebration?

"Of course," said McLain, as he made his way to the shower. "My house will be like a madhouse."

**NOT TILL THE FAT LADY SINGS 103**

**26**

THE DATE: March 27, 2005

THE LOCATION: Frank Erwin Center, Austin, Texas

THE SETUP:
In a classic NCAA tournament thriller against Kentucky in the Elite Eight, the Spartans survived a miracle triple from Patrick Sparks at the buzzer and two overtimes. For MSU coach Tom Izzo, the Final Four clincher was a ...

THE ELEMENTS

# Special delivery

JULIAN H. GONZALEZ/DETROIT FREE PRESS

Officials reviewed Patrick Sparks' late shot for about five minutes, eventually ruling it a three-pointer.

## By NICHOLAS J. COTSONIKA

**A**fter overcoming so much to make the Elite Eight — failure, criticism, self-doubt, Duke — Michigan State overcame even more to make the Final Four.

Kentucky scored a controversial, last-second three-pointer to force overtime, but MSU came back and won a classic, 94-88, in double overtime.

It led to its fourth Final Four appearance in seven years.

"After what these guys have been through, I think this was the most satisfying of all of them, maybe because I realized how hard it is to get back," said coach Tom Izzo, who had last gone to the Final Four in 2001. "This one, for me, it was special."

"It seemed like that shot hung on the rim forever. I was counting the seconds it was up there."

**TOM IZZO**, Michigan State coach, on Kentucky's last-second three-pointer that sent the game to overtime

DAVID P. GILKEY/DETROIT FREE PRESS

MSU's Kelvin Torbert, getting a hand from Matt Trannon, was in Partick Sparks' face when the Wildcat tied the game in regulation. Torbert got to breathe a sigh of relief later.

NOT TILL THE FAT LADY SINGS **105**

26

"It was a great game, one of the great moments. I was glad to be part of it, but I wasn't glad to be part of the wrong end."

**PATRICK SPARKS,** Kentucky guard, on losing to Michigan State in the 2005 NCAA tournament despite hitting a three-pointer that sent the game to overtime

DAVID P. GILKEY/DETROIT FREE PRESS

MSU point guard Drew Neitzel gets a souvenir after the Spartans' victory over Kentucky. MSU's run ended in the national semifinal against North Carolina.

Trailing in the final seconds of regulation, 75-72, the Wildcats started throwing up three-pointers. Patrick Sparks missed from the top of the key. Kelenna Azubuike missed from in front of the Kentucky bench.

Then, at the top of the key again, with Kelvin Torbert in his face, Sparks leaned forward and fired. Sparks said there was "a lot of contact," but there was no whistle.

The ball danced on the rim.

Slowly.

"It seemed like that shot hung on the rim forever," Izzo said. "I was counting the seconds it was up there."

Finally — after the horn sounded —

the ball fell through the hoop. Referee James Burr signaled a three-pointer, and the arena roared.

Sparks had gotten the shot off in time. But had he stepped on the arc?

He didn't even know.

"I didn't really know where my foot was," he said, "but I knew it was pretty close."

Burr went over to a video monitor. He said he asked for the replay to be blown up and took his time, because he "felt that the play was so important in deciding a college basketball game that was as great as that."

MSU fans chanted, "TWO! TWO!" Kentucky fans responded, "THREE! THREE!"

The Wildcats huddled.

"I was scared," Kentucky forward Chuck Hayes said.

"I was praying and hoping that, from the angle that they were seeing it from, it was a three-pointer. I didn't want it to end like that. I just knew that if they called it a three we had the momentum and were going to pull away in the first overtime."

The Spartans huddled, too.

"When they were trying to look at that shot, one of our coaches said, 'That's what we're here for. This is the drama,'" MSU center Paul Davis said.

Izzo said he approached his players

HARRY CABLUCK/ASSOCIATED PRESS

Patrick Sparks' toe is a whisker behind the three-point line as he sinks a triple at the buzzer. Sparks' shot sent the game to OT, setting the stage for the Spartans' own comeback.

JULIAN H. GONZALEZ/DETROIT FREE PRESS

Ravi Moss, right, shares Sparks' joy after his big shot, even as fans chanted, "TWO!" and "THREE!" while refs reviewed the play.

as if OT were certain.

"I just said, 'Hey, we beat them the first time, they made a heck of a play, give them credit. We're going to beat them a second time.' " Izzo said.

Finally, after about five minutes of tension, Burr signaled it was a three.

Overtime.

The stunned Spartans fell behind by four, but they rallied to tie. The game-saving sequence: Five straight missed shots by MSU followed by an offensive rebound. Then, Shannon Brown — who finished with a game-high 24 points and was named the Austin Regional's most out-

standing player — nailed a three-pointer to cut the deficit to one.

"We had the momentum in the first overtime," Sparks said, "and those offensive rebounds killed us."

Said Brown: "I think we just wanted to go out there and get the ball. We were trying to be relentless. I had a great look, and I put it in."

Overtime II.

The Spartans went ahead by six and held on. They made 11 of 12 free throws.

"It was a great game, one of the great moments," Sparks said. "I was glad to be part of it, but I wasn't glad to be part of the wrong end."

Then it was time to cut down the nets.

The Spartans — who beat top-seeded Duke the night before and were the first team to beat the Blue Devils and Wildcats in the same NCAA tournament — mobbed one another at center court with the cheerleaders and the mascot, Sparty.

Someone ran out with boxes of white caps and T-shirts. The players put them on, jumped up and down, wept and hugged.

"Double overtime, it's like, 'Damn. There's a lot going through my head,' " MSU's Alan Anderson said. "There's four teams left."

NOT TILL THE FAT LADY SINGS **107**

**THE DATE:** January 1, 1998

**THE LOCATION:** Rose Bowl, Pasadena, Calif.

**THE SETUP:**
Led by a QB with a comeback story and a cornerback with a Heisman Trophy, the Wolverines finally put the disappointments behind them. They took to the air, escaping before Washington State could take one last snap, finally able to say ...

**THE ELEMENTS**

# Hail, yes!

By MITCH ALBOM

The gun went off and the championship hats came on and oh, baby, it was really a happy new year now. Never mind that the last play of this crazy Rose Bowl may have been the craziest of all, with an all-world quarterback throwing the ball at his feet, then seeing 0:00 on the clock.

Never mind. This was a snapshot for history, a team of destiny, and nothing was going to stop the young men in maize and blue from the joyous celebration that awaited in the middle of the field.

All roses, no thorns.

National champions?

Hail, yes.

"We had to fight to the last second," said an exhausted Brian Griese, who was selected the game's most valuable player after his three touchdown passes led Michigan's 21-16 victory over Washington State, a victory that leaves the Wolverines 12-0 for the season and earns them a share of the national championship.

DAVID P. GILKEY/DETROIT FREE PRESS

U-M coach Lloyd Carr didn't mind being in the middle of a mob scene after winning the Rose Bowl.

"I never could have dreamed of an ending like this."

The ending? Who could have dreamed the beginning or the middle? Let's be honest. A Michigan national championship won on two long bombs is as likely as Metallica singing "White Christmas." As normal as Bo Schembechler in a Chippendales outfit.

Then again, it has taken 50 years for Wolverines fans to reach January saying, "We're undefeated and the best in the country." It's only fitting

"We had to fight to the last second.
I never could have dreamed of an ending like this."

**BRIAN GRIESE**, Michigan quarterback, on throwing three touchdown passes in a Rose Bowl MVP effort

"Football is a team game. Today we proved that team is No. 1 with us. And that we're the No. 1 team."

**CHARLES WOODSON**, Michigan cornerback, on beating Washington State by gaining nearly twice as many yards through the air than on the ground

JULIAN H. GONZALEZ/DETROIT FREE PRESS

> "We all felt we should be able to snap the ball and ground it in two seconds. But with all the confusion and the noise, I can't blame the officials."
>
> **RYAN LEAF**, Washington State quarterback, on the controversy surrounding the end of the game, which featured Leaf attempting to stop the clock with two seconds left, only to have time expire

DAVID P. GILKEY/DETROIT FREE PRES

Michigan's Tai Streets gets a boost from happy teammates after scoring a touchdown against Washington State in the 1998 Rose Bowl.

that they do it in style.

And that they did, here in glorious Pasadena, a place that has often resembled the valley of death for U-M football but more than made up for it in front of 101,219 screaming fans. What they saw flashed as many shades as the sun-drenched facade of the San Gabriel mountains. There were four lead changes, two interceptions, Michigan gaping at Washington State and its magnificent quarterback, Ryan Leaf, and the Cougars saying "Huh?" as Griese played bombs away with his receivers.

But in the end, U-M did what it does best, it held the ball for nearly seven minutes, then relied on its nation-leading defense to close the door. True, it did that with a gasp, as Leaf moved his Cougars 67 yards in 29 seconds, before the clock ran out as he intentionally grounded a pass.

"I never relaxed for one second," admitted coach Lloyd Carr, who was defensive coordinator in 1994 when Colorado tumbled Michigan on a final Hail Mary.

"I never want to relive that, let me tell you."

Not to worry, Lloyd.

All roses, no thorns.

Hail, yes.

"I don't know if I believe in fate, but I do believe in never giving up," said a smiling Griese, who, as a senior playing his last game, symbolized the unlikely ascension of this team. Here was a guy who walked on to the Michigan program as a freshman, who rose to starting quarterback, then fell as low as you can fall, being tossed off the team after an incident in a bar.

Day after day, as he trained on his own, running steps in a stadium while his teammates practiced elsewhere, one image kept him going. The image of him coming back one day, winning the big game, and showing everyone that he was not the bad kid the headlines suggested.

Mission accomplished. And how he did it! In the second quarter, with Michigan trailing, 7-0, he heaved a 53-yard bomb to Tai Streets that landed in his arms and woke up the previously dazed Michigan fans. It tied Griese's longest pass of the year.

And then, in case you didn't believe it the first time, the kid did it again — even better. This time it was the third quarter, right after Washington State had taken a jolting 13-7 lead, and Michigan fans were shivering, "uh-oh, not again."

No worries. Griese uncorked a 58-yarder down the middle, which floated on a wonderful arch and hit Streets in stride. Touchdown.

Streets, who endured dislocated fingers much of this season — which didn't stop fans from criticizing his ballhandling — had not caught a single pass in the two biggest games of the year: Penn State and Ohio State. Now he had two touchdowns?

"My fingers feel fine now," Streets said afterward.

He finished with four catches for 127 yards. He certainly would be the biggest story of this game — if not for Griese.

For in the final quarter, it was mostly the senior quarterback who saved the day, not only finding Jerame Tuman for a 23-yard touchdown but also steering a time-eating drive that chewed 6:56 off the clock. On one critical third down, Griese spun out of a tackler's grasp and chugged for a first down.

"I'm not the fastest guy in the world," he admitted, laughing at himself. But he needed 11 yards and he got 11 yards, diving for the final inch. He did it on an undying desire that has characterized his return to glory and shows that young men really can grow up at college, even when they play a game.

So when it was all over, and

JULIAN H. GONZALEZ/DETROIT FREE PRESS

Brian Griese earned Rose Bowl MVP honors, passing for three touchdowns and 251 yards.

Brian stood before the cheering crowd, the scoreboard suddenly flashed the image of his father, Bob, who was broadcasting the game for ABC-TV. And the senior Griese waved at his son, and all the bad times, all the blemishes, all those lonely training runs that once threatened to swallow Brian Griese were gone.

"I never wanted to be the all-star quarterback," he said. "I just want-

ed to be accepted on this team."

All roses, no thorns.

Now, speaking of all-star quarterbacks, a word here for Leaf. He made believers out of a lot of people. Against a defense that was only allowing 115 passing yards a game, Leaf racked up 331. He threw laser beams, held onto the ball until the absolute latest moment and took a pounding. He still almost pulled off a huge upset. With two seconds showing on the clock, he took the snap at Michigan's 26 and grounded the ball. He thought he'd given himself one last play.

Instead, to his disbelief, he looked up and saw the clock had expired.

"We all felt we should be able to snap the ball and ground it in two seconds," Leaf said. "But with all the confusion and the noise, I can't blame the officials. I

wouldn't want to have to keep track of time in that situation."

Who knows what might have happened with one more snap?

Anytime Michigan wins a game by gaining nearly twice as many yards passing as running, there must be some fate involved.

"Football is a team game," said U-M's Heisman Trophy winner, Charles Woodson, who had a key interception but was stymied offensively by WSU's defense.

"Today we proved that team is No. 1 with us. And that we're the No. 1 team."

The Wolverines came out here at No. 1, and they go home at No. 1.

"I am so proud of this team," said Carr.

All roses, no thorns.

Hail, yes.

Now that's how you start a new year.

## 28

**THE DATE:** December 27, 1953

**THE LOCATION:** Briggs Stadium, Detroit

**THE SETUP:**
Detroit's defense held legendary quarterback Otto Graham to four yards passing. But the Lions still trailed the Cleveland Browns, 16-10, late in the fourth quarter. That's when Jim Doran and Bobby Layne hooked up for a ...

# Championship connection

**By BOB LATSHAW**

**C**hampions win the close ones. It wouldn't have been closer or more dramatic as the Lions came from behind to capture their second straight world title. They defeated the Cleveland Browns, 17-16, before 54,577 delirious fans in Briggs Stadium in a brilliant exhibition.

Jim Doran snared a 33-yard scoring pass from Bobby Layne to give the Lions the victory.

Doran's catch came with two minutes left in the bruising championship playoff marked by flying fists that embroiled virtually every member of both squads.

Doran's touchdown — his only one of the year — erased a six-point deficit, and when Doak Walker kicked the extra point, Detroit became the third team to repeat as NFL champions.

Before the Lions scored, things looked dark for the Lions. Lou Groza had kicked three field goals — two in the fourth quarter — to give the Browns a 16-10 edge with less than five minutes left.

Although Doran scored the all-important touchdown, this was a team victory.

Detroit's defense stopped the peerless Otto Graham, who completed only two of 15 passes for four yards.

Even after Doran scored the winning touchdown, it was the defense that ended all hopes of a Browns comeback. Rookie Carl Karilivacz intercepted Graham, giving the Lions possession and an opportunity to kill the clock.

The Lions had raced to a 10-3 edge in the first quarter — thanks to a pair of mistakes by Graham. Then a Browns interception turned into a touchdown and the score was tied.

Groza kicked a 15-yard field goal after 44 seconds of play in the final period. After Walker missed a field goal from the 33, Groza booted what appeared to be the clincher from 43 yards out.

Groza did his best with the kickoff, booting it deep into the end zone. That gave Detroit the ball on its own 20. Then Layne and Doran went to work.

On the first play, Layne fired a pass to Doran for a first down on the Detroit 37. Two passes were incomplete, and it was third-and-10.

On this play, Layne picked out Doran again. The play was good for 18 yards and another first down. There was plenty of time left on the scoreboard clock — almost too much.

**Groza did his best with the kickoff, booting it deep into the end zone. That gave Detroit the ball on its own 20. Then Layne and Doran went to work.**

DETROIT FREE PRESS

Lions quarterback Bobby Layne ran a late drive to perfection in the 1953 NFL championship game against Cleveland.

**After a delay while various members of both teams swung punches, Layne stepped back, fired a perfect pass to Doran on the goal line, and Doran stepped over for six points.**

Cloyce Box was the next target — this time the advance was to the Browns' 36. Bob Hoernschemeyer was held to no gain on second down before Layne sneaked to the 33 for another first.

After a delay while various members of both teams swung punches, Layne stepped back, fired a perfect pass to Doran on the goal line, and Doran stepped over for six points.

That tied the game, and Walker was the man on the spot. He kicked his second extra point of the game, and Detroit held a slender one-point edge.

Karilivacz's interception made the single point stand.

In the winning drive, the Layne-Doran combination picked up 68 of the 80 yards.

**THE DATE:** October 14, 1984

**THE LOCATION:** Tiger Stadium, Detroit

**THE SETUP:**
Padres ace reliever Goose Gossage talked his manager out of it, convincing Dick Williams that he could get Tigers slugger Kirk Gibson out in a tense World Series moment that might prevent a return to San Diego. It ended up being a ...

THE ELEMENTS

# Poor decision, rich reward

### By GENE GUIDI

MARY SCHROEDER/DETROIT FREE PRESS

In 1979, Kirk Gibson first saw Goose Gossage's fastball. Make that, almost saw.

It was Gibson's first at-bat in the majors, and he struck out on three pitches against the Yankees right-hander.

Gossage threw the fastball to Gibson again, this time as a San Diego Padre, in Game 5 of the World Series. But this time the Tigers rightfielder saw it just fine, thank you. Gibson drove the pitch into the upper deck in rightfield for a three-run home run.

The mighty stroke turned a 5-4 nail-biter into an 8-4 bulge that assured the Tigers they would be world champions within the hour.

Not only did Gossage serve up the clinching homer, he also talked his manager out of walking Gibson intentionally.

"I wasn't surprised he pitched to me since I don't ever remember getting a hit off him in my life," Gibson said. "You know how I used to hit against him? I'd start swinging just about the time he was cranking up to throw."

But with runners on second and third, first base open and a right-handed hitter (Lance Parrish) com-

"I can't second-guess myself now. But I did apologize to Dick. What can I say? I felt confident I could get him out."
**GOOSE GOSSAGE**, on his decision to pitch to Tigers slugger Kirk Gibson, rather than walk him in Game 5 of the 1984 World Series

"I DON'T EVER
REMEMBER
GETTING
A HIT OFF
HIM IN MY LIFE."

**KIRK GIBSON**, on how he knew he'd get a pitch to hit in Game 5 of the 1984 World Series against Goose Gossage

MARY SCHROEDER/DETROIT FREE PRESS

JULIAN H. GONZALEZ/DETROIT FREE PRESS

Manager Sparky Anderson, middle, greeting Kirk Gibson after one of his two Game 5 homers, lost a bet to Gibson over whether Padres reliever Goose Gossage would pitch to him.

> **"Maybe most people don't go, but I'm not most people. It was 3-3 at the time, which is not when you're supposed to play scared."**
>
> **KIRK GIBSON**, on scoring from third on a 150-foot pop fly

ing up next, the strategy seemed to call for the intentional pass. Gibson insisted he knew that wasn't going to happen.

"I knew he wasn't going to put me on," Gibson said. "In fact, when I was in the on-deck circle I looked at Sparky (Anderson) in the dugout and held up 10 fingers, which was my signal that I'd bet him $10 Gossage

was going to pitch to me.

"Sparky nodded OK, that he would take the bet. He thought Gossage would walk me."

So did Padres manager Dick Williams. Williams had ordered Gossage to put Gibson on, but the relief ace called his manager to the mound and talked him out of it.

"I can't second-guess

myself now," Gossage said. "But I did apologize to Dick. What can I say? I felt confident I could get him out."

Gossage wasn't the only Padre who had trouble slowing Gibson down in Game 5. Gibson's first-inning homer off Mark Thurmond gave the Tigers a 2-0 lead.

And then, after San Diego had tied the game at 3 and was threatening to move the

PHOTOS BY MARY SCHROEDER/DETROIT FREE PRESS

Kirk Gibson may have slammed the door on the Padres in the World Series, but shortstop Alan Trammell, above, was named MVP. He had two homers and six RBIs in the Series.

Lance Parrish and the Tigers were the toast of Detroit after their victory in Game 5.

series West again, Gibson's other offensive dimension — his swiftness on the bases — turned a 150-foot pop-up into a sacrifice fly that put the Tigers ahead for good.

With Gibson on third and one out in the fifth, pinch-hitter Rusty Kuntz lifted a looper into short rightfield. Second baseman Alan Wiggins drifted back to make the catch, but his throw to the plate was late and off-line, and Gibson slid across to make it 4-3.

Gibson said third-base coach Alex Grammas told him to tag up.

But Gibson said he was going to head home even if he didn't get the go-ahead from Grammas.

"I'm an aggressive player," Gibson said. "Maybe most people don't go, but I'm not most people. It was 3-3 at the time, which is not when you're supposed to play scared."

As he was rounding third after he hit his second homer, he blew kisses to the crowd.

"These are the moments you've got to savor, man," he said.

NOT TILL THE FAT LADY SINGS **117**

**30**

THE SETUP:

As usual, Michigan faced Ohio State in a game that would determine the Big Ten title and a Rose Bowl berth. U-M battled back from a 14-6 halftime deficit and held a 26-24 lead with a minute to go. But victory wasn't secure until ...

THE ELEMENTS

# A kick went amiss

By **TOMMY GEORGE**

MARY SCHROEDER/DETROIT FREE PRESS

Quarterback Jim Harbaugh, celebrating with his father, Jack, guaranteed victory against Ohio State in 1986. He didn't fail on his promise.

**M**ichigan had been there before — no, not with quite the same setting or tremendous stakes — but this scenario was all too familiar.

Sixty-one precious seconds left. The ball floating and fluttering toward the goalposts and Michigan's lead in jeopardy, the Big Ten championship sailing from the Wolverines' grasp.

The roses were wilting.

But in the five seconds it took Ohio State's Matt Frantz to attempt a 45-yard field goal that had the distance but drifted left, several Wolverines pondered flashbacks and memories both sweet and sour.

Oh, how sweet this recollection will be: Michigan beat Ohio State, 26-24, before an Ohio Stadium-record crowd of 90,674.

Michigan and Ohio State tied for the Big Ten championship with 7-1 records, but the Wolverines earned the trip to the Rose Bowl against Arizona State on New Year's Day because they won the head-to-head battle with the Buckeyes. Ohio State ended up with a Cotton Bowl berth in Dallas.

And, in the end, the Wolverines' destiny was decided by one kick. One miss.

They had been there before.

"I've been there a lot," said Michigan coach Bo Schembechler, who got the game ball after his 166th U-M victory, passing Fielding H. Yost for most wins by a Michigan coach.

Schembechler vividly remembers this recent string of U-M games decided by late kicks, beginning with a loss at Iowa in 1985, and an Illinois

"I thought it would be good. I just knew it would be good. It felt good when I kicked it. I can't believe it."

**MATT FRANTZ**, Ohio State kicker, on his missed 45-yard field goal that would have given the Buckeyes a win and a Rose Bowl berth

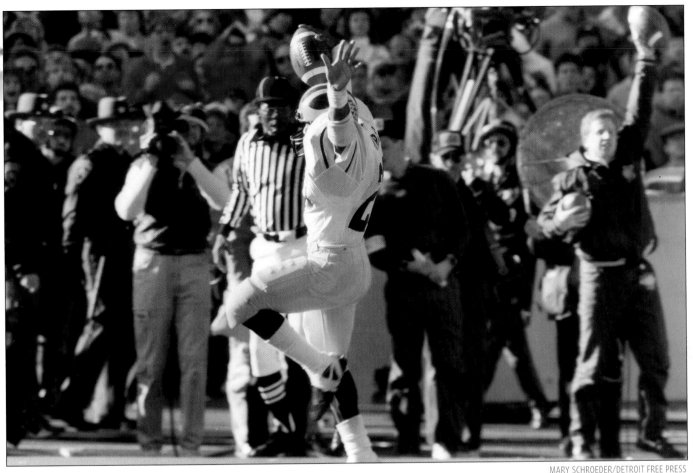

MARY SCHROEDER/DETROIT FREE PRESS

Michigan running back Jamie Morris rushes for a four-yard touchdown against Ohio State. He finished with two touchdowns and 210 rushing yards.

miss which finished that struggle in a tie.

The miss by Notre Dame in the final seconds of the season opener that saved U-M's win, the last-second boot over Iowa at Michigan Stadium, the game-ending boot by Minnesota that ended U-M's perfect season.

"We have been there before," quarterback Jim Harbaugh said. "We've seen it happen against us and for us. I was getting ready over there, if it went through, to try and drive us to get a field goal to win it."

Cornerback Garland Rivers was on the field during Frantz's kick, lining up deep and running hard for the block.

"I tried not to think about all the times before but just knock the ball down, and I almost got it," Rivers said. "I dove and looked up. And what did I see? I saw victory."

What Rivers and U-M's defense saw in OSU's first two offensive series was a punishing attack. It looked as if Michigan was in for more than it could handle.

The Buckeyes covered 125 yards in 13 plays on those two drives and led at halftime, 14-6.

But Michigan rebounded in the second half and finished with 529 yards of offense (268 rushing and 261 passing). U-M totaled 27 first downs, averaged

6.6 yards a play and won in possession time, 35:39 to 24:21.

Harbaugh and tailback Jamie Morris were the catalysts.

Harbaugh backed his guarantee of victory with 19-for-29 passing for 261 yards. Morris ran all over the Buckeyes, jolting for 210 yards on 29 carries, with two touchdown runs.

"Bo told us Thursday that he wanted us to run and play our best game ever, to play like we never have before, and then he came to my room last night and said there would be some creases and holes," Morris said. "We just had to find them."

Morris did.

But Frantz knew he could make up for Morris and all of Michigan's punch.

Especially when Thomas Wilcher fumbled at the OSU 37 with 3:17 left, setting up OSU's potential game-winning drive.

"I thought it would be good," Frantz said. "I just knew it would be good. It felt good when I kicked it. I can't believe it."

OSU coach Earle Bruce said: "If you saw it, there was nothing wrong with the kick. He kicked it hard and far, but sometimes you hook it, which is what happened. ... This is a tough game to lose, especially in Ohio Stadium. It's going to take awhile to get over this one."

"Bo told us Thursday that he wanted us to run and play our best game ever, to play like we never have before, and then he came to my room last night and said there would be some creases and holes."

**JAMIE MORRIS**, on the motivation he received from his coach

# Honorable mention

"It's pretty powerful when lots of different people step up."

**JOANNE P. McCALLIE**, Michigan State women's basketball coach, on her team's surprising run to the 2005 Final Four, which included a 16-point comeback in the national semifinal

**THE ELEMENTS**
Look for these eight elements in each of the 50 thrilling finishes:

**THE BIG COLLAPSE**

**THE BIG COMEBACK**

**CONTROVERSY STRIKES**

**THE HEART-BREAKER**

**1 HIGH STAKES**

**INDIVIDUAL EFFORT**

**VS THE BIG RIVALRY**

**TEAM EFFORT**

| Clash of the titans | **36** | The mother of all Big Ten shootouts | **37** | The Prince of defense | **38** | Role reversal | **39** | The Wings saw Red | **40** |
| Bartell's blunder | **46** | One for the ages | **47** | Dickie V's Titanic upset | **48** | Resilient to the very end | **49** | Birthday bonanza | **50** |

**THE DATE:** October 7, 1935

**THE LOCATION:** Navin Field, Detroit

**THE SETUP:**
Catcher-manager Mickey Cochrane knew Goose Goslin could bring Detroit its first title, so he traded for him. Tied, 3-3, with two outs in the bottom of the ninth in Game 6 of the World Series, Cochrane stood on second. And in the end, the ...

**THE ELEMENTS**

# Goose proves to be golden

### By CHARLES P. WARD

When Mickey Cochrane was made manager of the Tigers in 1933, his first official act was to make a trade with Washington, which brought the aging Goose Goslin to Detroit in exchange for young John Stone. Asked why he was willing to trade a youngster of great potential for a player who had seen his best days, Cochrane replied that a pennant-winning club had to have a player of the Goslin type in its lineup.

"The Goose is the kind of player who can win a pennant for you," he said, "and the World Series after you win the pennant. He's getting along in years, I'll admit, but he's good enough. I want him. He's a money player!"

The Tigers collected the profits

ASSOCIATED PRESS

Tigers catcher-manager Mickey Cochrane ended the 1935 World Series when he scored the winning run in the bottom of the ninth.

from that deal in Game 6 of the World Series, when Goslin produced the hit that scored Cochrane with the winning run in the ninth inning of

their game with the Chicago Cubs at Navin Field. The hit gave the Tigers a 4-3 win, gave Detroit its first world title and caused a crowd of 48,420 to swarm the field and stage one of the wildest celebrations in Detroit history.

The Goose's hit also helped Tommy Bridges win a bitter battle with Larry French, the Chicago southpaw. It was Bridges' second victory of the Series.

The teams were tied, 3-3, when the ninth inning opened, the Tigers having come from behind to tie the score in the sixth after the Cubs had moved ahead by scoring twice in the fifth.

Bridges had been touched for 11 hits during the first eight innings. And when Stanley Hack, Chicago's third baseman, tripled over the head of

**"The Goose is the kind of player who can win a pennant for you and the World Series after you win the pennant."**

**MICKEY COCHRANE,** on why he traded for aging hitter Goose Goslin before the 1934 season

ASSOCIATED PRESS

Goose Goslin's walk-off single in the bottom of the ninth scored Mickey Cochrane and set off a wild celebratory scene.

About that time, Old Red Gander stepped out of the batter's ring and into the box.

"Yea, Goose!" yelled youngsters in the bleachers. The Goose had gone to bat four times previously and had failed to get the ball out of the infield, but the youngsters didn't care. The Goose is the hero of the kids and "Yea, Goose!" is the cry they always give him when he steps up there in a pinch.

Soon the entire bleachers took up the cry. "Yea, Goose! Yea, Goose!" roared the jammed thousands as the Cubs' infield shifted to right and Herman moved way out on the grass to rightfield.

With the crowd's roars in his ears, the Goose swung hard at French's first pitch and lined a foul to right. French let go another and again the Goose swung.

This time the ball went on a line toward Herman. From the press box one couldn't tell whether Herman would be able to get his hands on the ball. He raced backward, leaped and then slumped back into a position that seemed to reflect dejection as the ball sailed over his head.

As a roar went up from the crowd, Cochrane tore for third, rounded the bag and headed homeward. Chuck Klein fielded the Goose's hit quickly and let go a throw to the plate. He had no chance of getting Cochrane, so Cavarretta cut off the throw glumly and headed for the clubhouse. The game was over. The Tigers were in.

**The Goose is the hero of the kids and "Yea, Goose!" is the cry they always give him when he steps up there in a pinch. Soon the entire bleachers took up the cry. "Yea, Goose! Yea, Goose!"**

Gerald Walker in center to open the Cubs' portion of the ninth, the fans began to reconcile themselves to the prospect of seeing the Series go the full seven games. Some even began to wonder whether the Tigers would let the title slip from their grasp just as they had in 1934 when the St. Louis Cardinals came from a 3-2 Series deficit to win. Everybody seemed to take it for granted that Hack would score.

But Bridges got Bill Jurges to strike out, French to hit an easy grounder back to the mound, and Augie Galan to hit an easy pop fly to Goslin, who gathered the ball in with a happy smile.

Then came the home half.

Flea Clifton worked the count to three balls and two strikes on French and then struck out.

Cochrane followed. He had made two hits in four previous trips, and French was careful in pitching to him. Not careful enough, however, for Cochrane hit a wicked bouncer toward right and was credited with a single when second baseman Billy Herman stopped the ball, but could-

n't hold it.

Charlie Gehringer followed Cochrane to the plate. Gehringer got two balls, and when French attempted to make the next pitch good, smashed a whistling drive toward first. Phil Cavarretta, Cubs' first sacker, didn't have much time to make up his mind what to do. But he dived in the direction of the ball, knocked it down, grabbed it and stepped on the bag. Gehringer was out but a looked-for double play on Cochrane didn't materialize. Cochrane reached second safely.

**32**

**THE DATE:** December 31, 1983

**THE LOCATION:** Candlestick Park, San Francisco

**THE SETUP:**
The Lions were a 43-yard kick away from the NFC championship game. And the owner of the longest field goal in playoff history was about to get a second chance from this shorter distance. Too bad all anyone will remember is ...

# Murray's bleepin' miss

By MIKE DOWNEY

**"D**id anybody say anything to you when you walked off the field?"

"I'm sure they said something lighter than what I was saying to myself," Eddie Murray said.

"What did you say to yourself?"

"I missed the (bleepin') kick," Murray said. "What can I say?"

Say, say, say what you want, but the football season is dead, Ed.

Happy bleepin' New Year.

It's like the wise old wide receiver Freddie (Doc) Scott said after what would be his final NFL game: "I feel I left all I had out there on the field. It's documented scientific fact that if things are traumatic, you don't forget them. We won't forget this game."

The Lions didn't leave their hurt in San Francisco.

They caught the first available flight after the super-sad 24-23 playoff loss to the 49ers. At the stroke of midnight they were sky-high, but only because they were on a plane.

It wasn't a new year for the Lions. It was the end of the year.

Too bad, too. They had the 49ers bent over, all ready to kick in the pants. They had Ready Eddie, Steady Eddie, the second-best Eddie Murray in professional sports lined up to kick the Lions right into the NFC championship game.

He already had hit the longest field goal in playoff history — 54 yards, just before halftime.

Later, Murray missed one from 43 yards, hooking it to the left. But when he got a second chance, from exactly the same distance, everybody in Candlestick Park was ready to light a candle for the 49ers.

"I even jumped up and started celebrating," said Murray's rarely overexcited coach, Monte Clark. "Even after he kicked it."

But Murray knew.

He knew the instant he kicked it that it was too wide to the right. It wasn't wide by much, but it was wide by enough.

"It's just like golf," Murray said, "where sometimes you try to hook the ball a little to bring it in, then realize you just should have slapped it right down the middle."

Said Gary Danielson, the holder: "The snap was good, the plant was good, and he kicked it straight as an arrow — an inch-and-a-half wide all the way."

Also as in golf, Murray said, he

---

**"I'm sure they said something lighter than what I was saying to myself. ... I missed the (bleepin') kick. What can I say?"**

**EDDIE MURRAY**, on missing a 43-yard field goal that would have sent the Lions to the NFC championship game

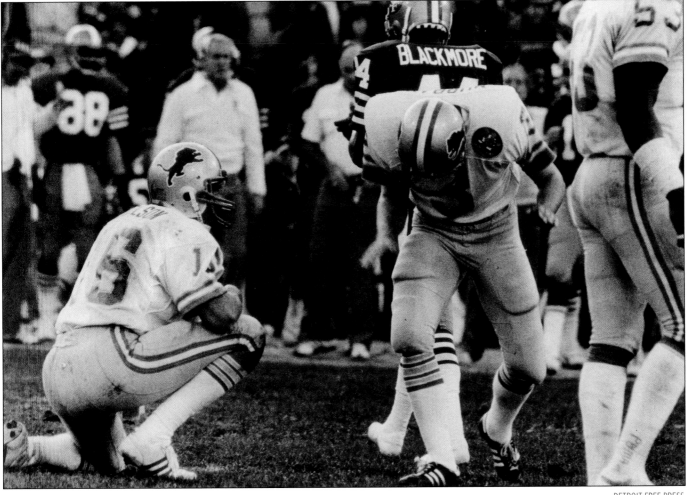

DETROIT FREE PRESS

Eddie Murray hangs his head after missing a last-second field goal in a playoff loss. Holder Gary Danielson said the plant and the hold were good.

often follows through to a certain spot, to the point where he doesn't have to watch the ball to tell which way it went. He said he didn't even have to look up to know he didn't hit it right.

Ray Wersching, the 49ers kicker, said he slipped every time he tried to kick. "The field was much softer and spongier than it appeared. I thought Murray was going to make it, but when he planted his left foot, it gave way, and I figured he might push it to the right. And he did."

"That could account for it," said Murray, "but I'm not going to say it. It didn't feel like I slipped. I don't want anything to sound like an excuse. I missed it. When I miss, I stand up and say I missed. And that's it."

But he thought about why he missed. He thought he "finessed" it and tried to aim it through the crossbars "instead of just kicking the hell out of it."

He thought he worried too much about it on the sidelines. In other words, he thought he thought about it too much.

And he's going to keep on thinking about it.

"I've missed game-winning kicks before, but not like this one," Murray said.

"I was always able to recoup the next week. This time I'm going to have all year to think about it.

"I know one thing: They're going to run it down my throat in the replays in Detroit. I'm just not going to be home to watch TV at 6 or 11 p.m. anymore, I guess."

A mob surrounded Murray, asking him what he thought, asking him how he felt.

"I'm sure everybody on the team is feeling what I'm feeling," he said.

"Unfortunately, they don't have everybody around their locker asking them about it."

Murray reached inside himself and found a smile. "I know you guys don't come to me when I do good," he said.

That's what happens when a guy gets to be so good. You come to expect his successes and be startled by his failures.

Nobody in the Lions' locker room had the nerve to say anything even remotely critical of Murray. They knew what he had done for them. They knew he was one of the reasons they had come this bleepin' far.

That, too, they would not forget. It's a documented scientific fact.

"It didn't feel like I slipped. I don't want any-thing to sound like an excuse. I missed it. When I miss, I stand up and say I missed. And that's it."

**EDDIE MURRAY**, refusing to say that a softer-than-expected field caused him to miss a poten-tial game-win-ning field goal in San Francisco

NOT TILL THE FAT LADY SINGS **125**

**33**

**THE SETUP:**
Linebacker Chris Spielman toiled eight seasons for the Lions, serving as witness to many crushing defeats for Detroit. But after Green Bay's last-minute Brett Favre to Sterling Sharpe touchdown pass, Spielman was ...

**THE ELEMENTS**

# The last man out

## By MITCH ALBOM

The Last Man Out pulled his coat on over his sweatshirt, and his hood up over his baseball cap. His jeans were zipped. His sneakers tied. He was ready to go, but he sat down anyhow.

As the few remaining players headed toward the exit, he bit a fingernail, nodded, and mumbled, "See ya tomorrow."

Then he caught himself.

"Listen to me," Chris Spielman said quietly, "I keep saying see ya tomorrow."

After the Lions' season ran out of tomorrows in a heart-squeezing, last-minute 28-24 defeat by Green Bay, some players dressed and left quickly. Some answered questions, and when the questions were finished, so were they.

Some nursed their aches and pains, and hobbled slowly to loved ones waiting in the tunnel.

They were all witnesses to Brett Favre's game-winning, 40-yard touchdown pass to Sterling Sharpe with 55 seconds remaining and Green Bay trailing by three points.

And Chris Spielman, who has long been the solar plexus of this team, took another shot to the gut. He stayed by his locker in the corner, the Last Man Out, as if maybe, if he waited long enough, some ref would come running in and yell, "It was all a mistake! Sharpe was out of bounds when he caught that touchdown! You guys won!"

Brett Favre was right on target when he delivered the game-winning, 40-yard touchdown pass to Sterling

Sharpe with 55 seconds remaining and Green Bay trailing by three points.

An hour passed. No ref. Instead, someone turned on a vacuum cleaner, and Spielman tried to talk over the whrrrrrrrrrrrrrrr.

"That feeling, when the ball was in the air, and you see the guy wide open in the end zone — it was one of the lowest feelings in the world. Your heart sinks. It's the closest thing there is to being told someone you love has died.

"I know people won't think its right to compare those things, but when you live and die for football, it is."

He rubbed his unshaven face and pushed his fingers through the hair behind his ears. The vacuum was near his locker now, whirring away, and he shook his head in the noise.

---

**"That feeling, when the ball was in the air, and you see the guy wide open in the end zone — it was one of the lowest feelings in the world."**

**CHRIS SPIELMAN**, Lions linebacker on his emotions when Green Bay completed a game-winning touchdown pass in the 1994 playoffs

JULIAN H. GONZALEZ/DETROIT FREE PRESS

Linebacker Chris Spielman played with the Lions from 1988-1995. The Lions were 1-4 in the playoffs in that span.

Spielman will be in the Silverdome later on in the week, by himself, lifting weights, getting sweaty, because he admits he is addicted to this game.

And yet even he has adapted. After the game, I asked his plans for the week.

"Wednesday night I start Lamaze class with my wife," he said. "She's eight months pregnant."

Lamaze class? Chris Spielman?

"I know, I know," he said, chuckling softly. "But I've changed. Besides, I always promised if I ever had a family, it would come first, so I'm gonna stick by that."

Maybe there's a lesson there. We can go with the old ways, kick and moan about these luckless Lions, or we can adjust with age, admit that at times this team stunk, and at times it really surprised us, and it did win the Central Division, and, good or bad, it gave us more to talk about than any other Detroit team all year.

Choose your poison. As Spielman headed for the door, a public relations man yelled over, "It's locked, Chris! You can't go out that way."

They can't go out that way. But year after year they do. These Lions. You make peace, or you drive yourself crazy.

"See ya tomorrow," Spielman said instinctively. And he pushed through the door to meet his pregnant wife because, eventually, life does go on, win or lose, for everyone, even the Last Man Out.

> "It's the closest thing there is to being told some-one you love has died. I know people won't think it's right to compare those things, but when you live and die for football, it is."
>
> **CHRIS SPIELMAN**, on how crushed he was by losing in the playoffs again

Doesn't it always seem to end like this? A Lions season? With some sort of heartbreak? Even in the playoffs? If it isn't Eddie Murray missing a field goal against San Francisco, it's the Washington Redskins scoring their umpteenth touchdown against the Lions or, with a minute left, Kevin Scott, slowing up, as if driving past an accident scene,

while Sterling Sharpe sneaks behind him into the end zone and catches a bomb pass right out of the sandlot.

There were theories offered from doughnut shops to radio talk shows, theories as to why you shouldn't feel bad about the Lions' playoff exit:

1) They would have lost to the 49ers anyhow

2) They would have got-

ten killed by the 49ers.

3) They were lucky to be in the playoffs.

4) What did you expect from coach Wayne Fontes?

None of these are necessarily true. None of them really makes you feel better. But in their own weird way, they are part of the healing process.

Talk it out. Assign blame. Wrap up the season before you stick it in the attic.

# 34

**THE DATE:** June 11, 1998

**THE LOCATION:** Joe Louis Arena, Detroit

**THE SETUP:**
The Wings trailed the Washington Capitals by two in the third period of Game 2 of the Stanley Cup finals. But something kept a Cap from scoring on an open net, and two unlikely Wings scored to tie and win the game. Victory came ...

**THE ELEMENTS**

# By wings of angels

GABRIEL B. TAIT/DETROIT FREE PRESS

**By MITCH ALBOM**

**S**omebody get the name of that angel. The one that blew a loose puck away from an open Detroit net, the one who threw a bag full of pixie dust on Steve Yzerman's uniform, the one who snuck Kris Draper onto the ice and made him turn and fire a goal with 4:36 left in overtime that switched what seemed like a sure defeat in the Stanley Cup finals into yet another notch on the Red Wings' amazing victory belt.

"It's what you dream about as a kid playing rubber-ball hockey," said Draper, whose goal capped a 5-4 comeback victory to give the Wings a 2-0 lead in the finals. "Clock winding down, you take the shot to win the game. I think my smile tells you how I feel about it."

Wow! What a night! In a three-hour, 31-minute marathon, under a rain of noise by a near-crazed Joe Louis Arena crowd, the Wings proved that this series might be about fate after all. It would be hard to explain how they came back from 3-1 and 4-2 deficits to win without a little magic mixed in.

It might be even harder to explain the normally unflappable Scotty Bowman smiling and pumping his fist.

This was more than a hockey game. It was pandemonium unleashed, three goals in less

"I think if you threw all the names in a hat, mine would have been the last one you pulled out. But I'll take it."

**KRIS DRAPER**, commenting on the unlikeliness of scoring the winning goal in overtime of Game 2 of the 1998 Stanley Cup finals

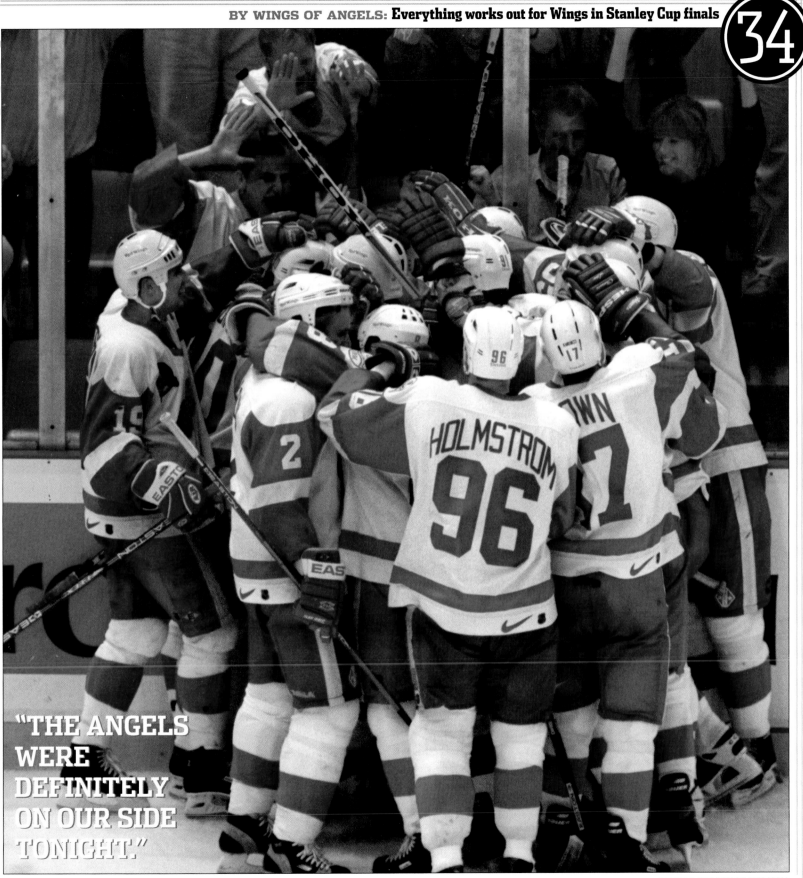

"THE ANGELS WERE DEFINITELY ON OUR SIDE TONIGHT."

**MARTIN LaPOINTE,** on the Wings' unlikely comeback from a two-goal deficit in Game 2 of the 1998 Stanley Cup finals.

GABRIEL B. TAIT/DETROIT FREE PRESS

"It's what you dream about as a kid playing rubber-ball hockey. Clock winding down, you take the shot to win the game. I think my smile tells you how I feel about it."

**KRIS DRAPER**, on scoring the winning goal in overtime of Game 2 of the 1998 Stanley Cup finals

JULIAN H. GONZALEZ/DETROIT FREE PRESS

Wings goalie Chris Osgood stops Esa Tikkanen's shot in the second period. Tikkanen would later blow a big opportunity to put the game away for the Caps.

than 10 minutes by Washington, and three goals in less than nine minutes by Detroit. But mostly, it was about putting your head down and coming back from long odds, never quitting. It was all about second effort, like Yzerman following up his first shot and scoring on the rebound, like Doug Brown ignoring misses on earlier chances and putting in the game-tying goal with just less than five minutes to go in the third period. Like Draper, who hadn't scored a goal in the 1998 playoffs, hanging in until his chance came on a perfect crossing pass by Martin Lapointe.

Red Wings enforcer Joey Kocur, right, tangles with Washington's Esa Tikkanen, as Washington goalie Olaf Kolzig looks on.

GABRIEL B. TAIT/DETROIT FREE PRESS

"I think if you threw all the names in a hat," Draper said, laughing, "mine would have been the last one you pulled out. But I'll take it."

It was a night of broken sticks and body slams, a night when the Capitals peppered Chris Osgood with pucks, and a night when Osgood actually threw one back. It was noise and chills and drama and shrieks — a typical overtime NHL playoff game. It left the Capitals shaking their heads and the Wings rolling their eyes. Detroit fired 60 shots on Olaf Kolzig and came back from weighty deficits.

Then again, none of this whooping and celebrating would be taking place if Esa Tikkanen hadn't gone temporarily blind and dizzy late in the game, when he stole an Yzerman pass and faked Osgood into a flop. The net was wide open. The scorer had his finger on the button. It was a chipper, a no-brainer, like letting water go down the tub. A simple flip for a two-goal lead.

Tikkanen missed.

"The angels were definitely on our side tonight," said a grinning Lapointe.

What can you say about these Red Wings? No team in 42 years had come back to win in the finals after trailing by two goals in the third period. This Detroit squad seems to breathe in and out, right before your eyes, absorbing a blow like a cagey old fighter, knowing that nothing counts until the final bell.

So here were the Wings, in the third period, down two goals, and down a player on a Washington power play. The crowd was on the edge of despair, and fans were squirming with the idea that Detroit, for the first time since 1995,

KIRTHMON F. DOZIER/DETROIT FREE PRESS

Red Wing Doug Brown rejoices after beating Capitals goalie Olaf Kolzig to tie the game in the third period of Game 2.

would lose a game in the finals.

And then along came the captain. Yzerman took a breakaway pass and raced down the ice, dangling the puck between sharing and scoring, just long enough to get the lone defenseman to leave an opening. Then Yzerman fired right through Kolzig, a shot hard enough to cut through the back of the net.

And suddenly the arena was a revival meeting, people screaming "I believe! I believe!"

They believed. Even when Washington scored on that same power play 28 seconds later, they believed. And when Lapointe took an Igor Larionov feed and spun and hit pay dirt, they believed even more.

And when Brown fired high

over Kolzig and saw the red light flash, they believed even more. Brown did a midair dance, pumping his fists as he spun around.

He believed. They believed. The whole building believed. And when Draper fired and Bowman shook his fist, well, wouldn't you believe, too?

**35**

THE SETUP:
As 2000 wound to a close, the Lions were poised to reach the playoffs. All that remained was to beat the 4-11 Bears on Christmas Eve. Although the Lions took an early lead, there would be no Merry Christmas for Lions fans. It was ...

THE ELEMENTS

# Bah, humbug!

BY CURT SYLVESTER

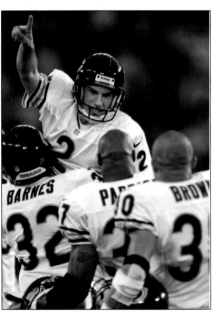

DAVID P. GILKEY/DETROIT FREE PRESS

Former MSU kicker Paul Edinger gets a hero's ride off the field from his Bears teammates after booting the Lions from playoff contention with a 54-yard field goal with two seconds left.

They really outdid themselves this time.

In their long and distinguished history of disappointing losses, the Lions staged a real doozy. On Christmas Eve. On their home field. Against a team that finished the season with a 5-11 record.

With the playoffs just a victory away, the Lions let the Chicago Bears get away with an agonizing 23-20 win that finished them for the season and sent their Silverdome crowd of 71,957 home in despair. Again.

Rookie kicker Paul Edinger from Michigan State did the dirty work with a 54-yard line drive field goal that broke the tie at 20 with just two seconds to play, leaving the Lions dazed and disappointed. Again.

The loss dropped them to 9-7 and fourth place in the NFC Central Division; the Bears finished in fifth.

To say it was shocking would be an understatement.

The Lions expected the Bears to play the spoiler role to the hilt, but they also expected to spend Christmas Day putting together playoff plans, preparing for a first-round game at Philadelphia or New Orleans.

"These games you've got to win," coach Gary Moeller said. "I mean, you've got to win these games. When you're supposed to win, you've got to win.

"But that's the NFL. That happens more often than we would like to think but, hey, I'm the head coach, too. And I've got to figure out a way to help them win."

"These games you've got to win. I mean, you've got to win these games. When you're supposed to win, you've got to win."
**GARY MOELLER**, Lions coach, after a loss to the 4-11 Bears kept the Lions from qualifying for the playoffs

"I OBVIOUSLY DIDN'T KNOW SOMEBODY WAS THAT CLOSE TO ME."

JULIAN H. GONZALEZ/DETROIT FREE PRESS

**STONEY CASE,** on his fumble late in the game as he attempted to lead the Lions to a winning score

DAVID P. GILKEY/DETROIT FREE PRESS

Luther Elliss, left, and J.B. Brown can't bear to watch the bitter end of the 2000 season.

"We really deser-ved it, the fans deser-ved it, the city deser-ved it, and for it not to happen is going to linger for a long time in the off-season."

**JOHNNIE MORTON**, Lions wide receiver, on the pain of missing the playoffs unexpectedly

JULIAN H. GONZALEZ/DETROIT FREE PRESS

The Lions' loss to the Bears marked the end of Gary Moeller's coaching career in Detroit. About a month later, the Matt Millen era began.

Instead, the Lions found a way to lose. Again.

They did it with dropped passes, interceptions and fumbles, and by failing to take advantage of their opportunities.

It wasn't as though the Lions didn't have their chances. They took a 10-0 lead on Jason Hanson's 41-yard field goal and Charlie Batch's nine-yard touch-down pass to David Sloan, all in the first 8:08 of the game.

That's when the Bears were supposed to come unglued, as any self-respect-ing team with just four wins in its first 15 games would

do. Instead, they got tougher, and it was the Lions' playoff hopes that began to unravel.

Wide receiver Herman Moore dropped a pass for what might have been a 53-yard touchdown early in the second quarter when he lost the ball in the lights.

Batch hit a wild streak — misfiring on six of his next seven throws — and then took a jolt to his ribs from blitzing Bears rookie line-backer Brian Urlacher that finished him for the day.

It became Stoney Case's game the rest of the way, and the Lions backup quar-terback had a roller-coaster

JULIAN H. GONZALEZ/DETROIT FREE PRESS

Lions quarterback Charlie Batch looks on in disappointment. He suffered a rib injury, courtesy of rookie Brian Urlacher, late in the first half and never returned.

ride that ended with a crash.

Case scored on a 13-yard quarterback draw at 11:14 of the fourth quarter to regain the lead for the Lions, 17-13, but several minutes later Bears cornerback R. W. McQuarters intercepted a Case pass and returned it 61 yards for a touchdown.

And when Case tried to rally the Lions to victory in the closing minutes after they had tied the game on Hanson's 26-yard field goal with 1:56 to play, he was hit by McQuarters, fumbled and the Bears recovered just beyond midfield, setting up Edinger's game-winning field goal.

In hindsight, Case said he regretted not pulling the ball down and scrambling instead of scrambling and trying to throw.

"I was close (to running), but I had some guys open downfield that would have been a big play," Case said. "I obviously didn't know somebody was that close to me."

It was not as though Case lost the game single-handedly, however.

The Lions' defense, which had stood tall in the previous Sunday's 10-7 victory against

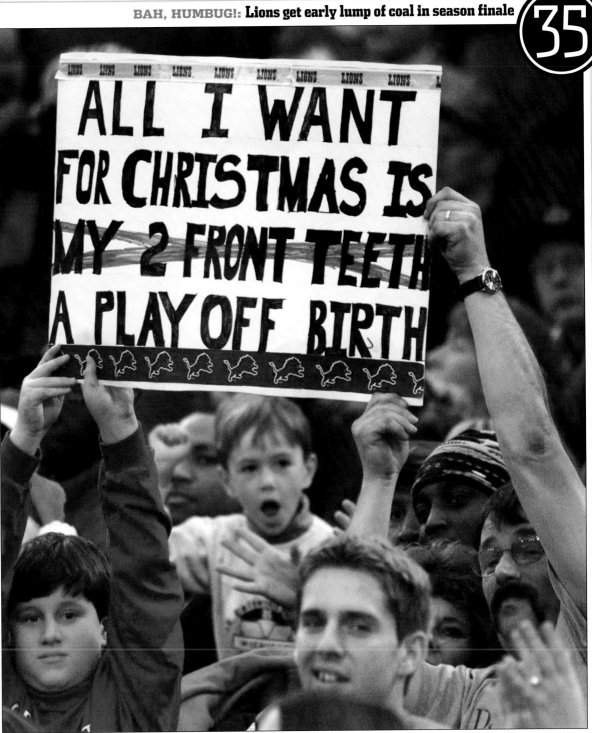

JULIAN H. GONZALEZ/DETROIT FREE PRESS

Santa Claus didn't grant the wish of these Lions fans. As usual, it was a lump of coal for Detroit.

the New York Jets at the Meadowlands, was victimized by Shane Matthews on a 59-yard drive that set up the second of Edinger's three field goals, a 50-yarder.

And the Bears ripped through the Lions' defense on a 90-yard

drive that gave them the lead at the Silverdome with backup quarterback Cade McNown completing a 27-yard touchdown pass to wide receiver Marty Booker.

"We really deserved it, the fans deserved it, the city

deserved it, and for it not to happen is going to linger for a long time in the off-season," receiver Johnnie Morton said.

Or, as Ebenezer Scrooge put it about 150 years ago in the Charles Dickens classic: "Bah, humbug!"

## 36

**THE DATE:** April 27, 1984

**THE LOCATION:** Joe Louis Arena, Detroit

**THE SETUP:**
Tied at two victories apiece, the Pistons battled the Knicks in Game 5 for a chance to move into the second round of the NBA playoffs. Isiah Thomas and Bernard King put on a show. It was an unforgettable ...

# Clash of the titans

BY MIKE DOWNEY

Joe, it was a night you would have been proud to have your name on the building.

It was a knockout of a night, a blast from the past, a fight to the finish.

The Pistons fought and fought at your arena, Joe Louis, until they were ready to drop, and that's eventually what they did, 127-123. It was the final round of an NBA playoff rumble with the New York Knicks, and Joe, it was a night to remember.

It was a night when the Pistons came back to Detroit because the Pontiac Silverdome was booked with a motocross event, a night when urban ball replaced suburban ball, a night when a bunch of guys shooting baskets turned 21,208 men, women and children into basket cases.

It was the night the Pistons and Knicks worked overtime to see who'd survive, winner take all, with the Boston Celtics in the wings.

It was a night of living dangerously.

When Isiah Thomas hit New York in the heart with a three-point shot, 23 seconds from the end of regulation, it looked like Detroit's night.

When Trent Tucker of the Knicks broke free to the basket as time ran out, it looked like New York's night.

More than anything, it was a night everyone would not soon forget.

"First of all, the sun's going to come up tomorrow," Terry Tyler said. "But it'll be awhile before we forget this one."

"You can say we were satisfied with how we did this season," Earl Cureton said, "except that until you win it all, hit the peak, you're never really satisfied."

"I know I'll never forget this game," Kelly Tripucka said. "I can live without the way it turned out, but, otherwise, it was a hell of a night."

It was a night when maybe three times as many black basketball fans came around than had come to a typical game at the Silverdome.

It was a night with a crowd so big, you'd have thought Frank Sinatra and Eddie Murphy were appearing in concert dressed like Boy George.

And what a game it was, with the Pistons leading the Knicks from the start, then chasing them all the way to the finish.

"Everybody on both sides gave it all they had," Thomas said. "Even Mike (Abdenour) the trainer was good out there tonight."

It was a night Mayor Coleman

---

**"I know I'll never forget this game. I can live without the way it turned out but, otherwise, it was a hell of a night."**
KELLY TRIPUCKA, on his feelings after losing, 127-123, to the Knicks in Game 5 of the first round of the 1984 NBA playoffs

DETROIT FREE PRESS

The Knicks' Bernard King finished with 44 points, beating Isiah Thomas by four in one of the NBA's classic duels.

there would be no more games to take.

This was it for the Pistons — tied at two wins apiece with the Knicks in a best-of-five series.

There was enough fire in their eyes to roast marshmallows over them. There was so much noise in the air, it was like a building full of 21,000 Dick Vitales.

"And it was so hot," coach Chuck Daly said. "Is it always so hot in here?"

(No. If it was, several Red Wings would drown.)

Daly didn't lose his cool. The coach looked up and down his bench and picked out Ray Tolbert and Lionel Hollins and other players who rarely play. If this was going to be the final night of his first year, Daly was going to go out the way he came in: making sure the Pistons played as a team.

He stood in front of his bench, immaculate in a double-breasted suit.

Hubie Brown stood in front of his bench down the way, stripped to his shirtsleeves, pacing like a father in the maternity ward. That's what kind of night it was.

It was a night so wild and rowdy that when the Pistons put on a show of pregame slams and jams, one of them shook the backboard so much that a red lightbulb (indicating fouls), suspended from the 24-second clock, crashed to the court and shattered.

That was the beginning. And by the end, the weary, the beaten, the deserving-better Pistons themselves had been shattered, and the season was over.

Say it isn't so, Joe, say it isn't so.

"Everybody on both sides gave it all they had. Even Mike (Abdenour) the trainer was good out there tonight."

**ISIAH THOMAS**, who in one stretch scored 16 of his 40 points in 65 seconds, helping to force overtime

Young came to a game in the city he runs, and Mike Ilitch came to a game in the arena where his Red Wings play, and Bill Bonds came to a game to get the news firsthand, and Ricardo Montalban came to a game to help Detroiters live out their fantasy.

It was a night where standing-room-only fans encircled every inch of the stadium, where the sitting-room fans occupied every sticky staircase, where the city's fire inspector would have had a coronary if anyone had even threatened to strike a match.

It was more than a crowd. It was a crowd and a half.

Because it was more than a game. It was a war on a floor.

It was professional basketball at its best and worst and absolute baddest.

Playoff basketball — played by men who would scare the Guardian Angels right off the subways. Men from New York and Detroit, who aren't afraid of anything.

It was a night when no fewer than seven players with taped-up, dislocated

fingers played a game that requires dexterity and sleight of hand like no other.

It was a night when Bernard King of the Knicks and Cliff Levingston of the Pistons locked elbows and bumped hips and gave each other spinal massages.

It was a night when Tripucka went flying into the photographers after chasing a player to the hoop, and Kent Benson went sprawling over the scorer's table after a loose ball, because if they didn't take this night's game,

NOT TILL THE FAT LADY SINGS **137**

**THE DATE:** November 4, 2000

**THE LOCATION:** Ryan Field, Evanston, Ill.

**THE SETUP:**

On this night, Michigan and Northwestern combined for 1,189 yards of offense. Finally, a break: The Wolverines had the ball and a five-point lead with 1:38 left. But an Anthony Thomas fumble set up a 54-51 Wildcats win in ...

**THE ELEMENTS**

# The mother of all Big Ten shootouts

BY MICHAEL ROSENBERG

It was the wildest game in Michigan history. And as far as U-M's defense was concerned, it was the worst.

Northwestern piled up 654 yards of offense — 332 on the ground — to beat Michigan, 54-51.

Damien Anderson ran for 268 yards for the Wildcats — and dropped a pass that nearly cost his team the game. Anthony Thomas ran for 199 yards for the Wolverines — and fumbled in the final minute as he was trying to seal the game for U-M.

Thomas' fumble, with Michigan leading, 51-46, was recovered by Raheem Covington of Northwestern with 46 seconds left. Three plays later, Zak Kustok hit Sam Simmons for an 11-yard touchdown, and

Kustok hit Teddy Johnson for the two-point conversion to make it 54-51.

U-M's last-second attempt at a 57-yard field goal was ruined by a botched snap.

Thomas' fumble came after Anderson dropped a pass in the end zone on fourth down, which would have given Northwestern the lead.

So all Michigan had to do was run off 1:38 of time.

"I tried to take a little bit too much and some bad things happened," Thomas said.

But Thomas' play, while obviously crucial, was not U-M's problem. A bigger concern was its awful defense.

Northwestern's 654 yards snapped a month-old record by a Michigan opponent. On Oct. 7, Purdue ran up 530 yards in a 32-31 upset of

Michigan. In both games, U-M had a 28-10 lead before losing.

Nobody in the country has had a month like Michigan: second-worst defensive performance in school history, shutout, shutout, worst defensive performance in school history.

The loss overshadowed a phenomenal U-M offensive performance. Michigan gained 535 yards, which was 119 fewer than Northwestern, but that's misleading. The Wolverines simply had better field position than the Wildcats.

Both teams were scoring on virtually every possession.

"If you don't tackle, you'll have problems with any offense," U-M coach Lloyd Carr said.

"Right from the very beginning the tackling was very shoddy. I didn't see that it ever changed. We just did not

**"There were two very good offensive teams out there tonight, and it looked to me like two very poor defensive teams."**

LLOYD CARR, Michigan coach, commenting on the 1,189 yards of offense and 105 points between the teams

get many people to the football."

What resulted looked more like pinball than football. David Terrell and Thomas each scored three touchdowns. Bill Seymour scored the other for Michigan, and Hayden Epstein drilled a 52-yard field goal.

But Anderson scored four times, Kustok scored twice and Simmons and David Farman each caught touchdown passes.

U-M's Drew Henson completed 23 of 35 passes for 312 yards and four scores. He also fumbled once. Walker and Terrell each caught nine passes, Marquise Walker for 134 yards and Terrell for 117.

In this shootout, Northwestern even bought itself an extra possession with a brilliantly executed onside kick.

"There were two very good offensive teams out there tonight, and it looked to me like two very poor defensive teams," Carr said.

The winning coach saw it differently, of course.

"I've been coaching for 25 years, and I don't know if I've ever seen a more courageous, inspiring performance," Northwestern coach Randy Walker said. "We just keep finding a way to win."

> "I tried to take a little bit too much and some bad things happened."
>
> **ANTHONY THOMAS,** on his last-minute fumble that allowed Northwestern to beat Michigan in 2000

STEPHEN J. CARRERA/ASSOCIATED PRESS

Northwestern quarterback Zak Kustok tossed an 11-yard touchdown pass with 20 seconds left to beat Michigan.

**38**

THE DATE: May 24, 2004

THE LOCATION: Conseco Fieldhouse, Indianapolis

THE SETUP:
In Game 2 of the Eastern Conference finals, the Pistons' defense came to the rescue against Indiana. But it was one defensive play that stopped the Pacers from taking control of the series. It allowed Tayshaun Prince to be crowned ...

THE ELEMENTS

# The Prince of Defense

BY DREW SHARP

**A**s if swatting away an incredible 19 shots didn't already validate an impressive defensive exhibition, the Pistons saved the most sparkling display for last.

The Pistons were unraveling. A seemingly safe six-point lead was quickly evaporating.

Reggie Miller scooped up the loose ball after another turnover. He had a clear path to the basket and an uncontested lay-up to tie the game.

But then it came out of nowhere.

It was neither bird nor plane, but considering the magnitude of the deed, Tayshaun Prince should have been fitted for a red cape.

He flew 94 feet, swooping down upon the unsuspecting Miller, not

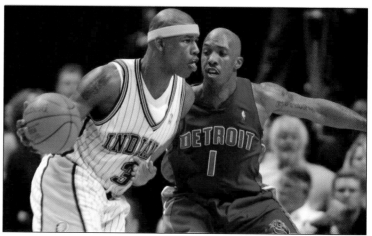

KIRTHMON F. DOZIER/DETROIT FREE PRESS

Tight man-to-man defense was the norm for Chauncey Billups and the Pistons in their rough series against Al Harrington and the Pacers.

only blocking the shot, but incredibly keeping the ball inbounds as he sailed into a pit of cameramen.

"I just kept running," Prince said. "I wasn't sure if I was going to get

there in time, but I didn't want to give up on the play."

The word "hustle" gets tossed around quite easily, but it found a definition in that one moment. The

*"Reggie probably thought that he was going to get an easy one, but I saw Tayshaun running up behind him. That was one of the best plays I ever saw. Tayshaun didn't give up on it."*

**BEN WALLACE**, on Tayshaun Prince's block of Reggie Miller in the fourth quarter

"I WASN'T SURE IF I WAS GOING TO GET THERE IN TIME, BUT I DIDN'T WANT TO GIVE UP ON THE PLAY."

**TAYSHAUN PRINCE,** on preventing a lay-up that would have tied the game with his block of Reggie Miller

KIRTHMON F. DOZIER/DETROIT FREE PRESS

NOT TILL THE FAT LADY SINGS **141**

"I'm familiar with seeing Tayshaun make plays like that. He's so long and athletic. It was a great effort, and it just shows you how much everybody's putting out."

**RICK CARLISLE,** Indiana coach, and former Pistons coach, on Prince's block of Reggie Miller

KIRTHMON F. DOZIER/DETROIT FREE PRESS

Mehmet Okur rejects Jermaine O'Neal, one of the Pistons' 19 blocks in Game 2.

blueprint of this Pistons' victory was the strained contortion on Prince's face after he was helped back to his feet. It was the look of determination fighting through fatigue.

Prince's play proved symbolic. It represented an evening in which nothing came easily.

No easy shots. No easy victories.

Indiana produced only 24 points in the second half. Roll that number around in your head for a bit. Twenty-four points in two quarters!

And yet the Pistons still needed one of the greatest defensive plays you'll ever see in the concluding seconds of a playoff game to pull out a 72-67 victory.

"Reggie probably thought that he was going to get an easy one, but I saw Tayshaun running up behind him," said Ben Wallace. "That was one of the best plays I ever saw. Tayshaun didn't give up on it."

Miller said that he saw Prince in his rearview mirror and in hindsight should have dunked it. But, quite honestly, he didn't think it was possible for Prince to make any play.

Nobody did.

And now nobody can question Prince's determination. The final line in the box score — five points, five rebounds, four blocks — didn't seem overly dazzling, but he helped frustrate the Pacers' emotional fulcrum, Ron Artest, into perhaps his worst playoff performance.

"Tayshaun made one of the greatest hustle plays I've ever seen," said coach Larry Brown. "We lost our poise and things looked like they were falling apart, and he stepped up and made a great play. It was a great overall team defensive effort. We did a very good job of contesting their shots."

Rasheed Wallace razzes the Pacers' crowd after the Pistons upheld his GuaranSheed of a win in Game 2. The Pistons won the series in six games en route to the NBA title.

Rasheed Wallace guaranteed a Piston victory in Game 2. He should have promised that the winner would score 80 points. But he's smart enough to realize that assuring the win would be easier.

"We had 'Sheed's back tonight," said Richard Hamilton. "We were confident that if we played a tough defensive game that our chances of winning would be pretty good."

It's obvious through only two games that toughness will be as much of a predictor of achievement as talent. There won't be much scoring and, as a result, six-point leads will be the equivalent of double-digit advantages in previous series.

The Pacers established a number of playoff career lows. The Pistons started as though they would challenge historical standards for futility. Five minutes into the game, they had as many turnovers (three) as points.

And those who adore at least a shade of offensive skill are no doubt prepared to take a club to this series. But Prince's game-saving resolve validated what unfolded on the floor. The great defensive play can leave you shaking your head in disbelief the same as the magnificent offensive moment.

"That was the play of the game for them," said Indiana coach Rick Carlisle. "I'm familiar with seeing Tayshaun make plays like that. He's so long and athletic. It was a great effort, and it just shows you how much everybody's putting out. It was a grueling game."

**THE DATE:** September 16, 1981

**THE LOCATION:** Caesars Palace, Las Vegas

**THE SETUP:**

Detroit's Thomas (Hit Man) Hearns would win seven world titles. But his first battle with Sugar Ray Leonard was his first time in the spotlight. Leonard, the classic boxer, outslugged the big-hitting Hearns. It was ...

THE ELEMENTS

# Role reversal

### By GEORGE PUSCAS

**S**ugar Ray Leonard, in a strange role reversal, turned slugger and battered Detroit's Thomas (Hit Man) Hearns into a 14th-round technical knockout in a raging struggle for the undisputed world welterweight boxing championship.

A sellout throng of 24,083 at the Caesars Palace Sports Pavilion, and millions more at television outlets around the world, saw Hearns suffer his first defeat even as he led significantly on all three judges' cards.

"I definitely knew I was ahead," Hearns said, "but there was just one problem. I got hit with a good shot. I thought I was in pretty good control (of my senses), but the ref didn't, and there's nothing I can do."

HUGH GRANNUM/DETROIT FREE PRESS

Thomas Hearns, right, posing with Hilmer Kenty in his early days, began 32-0 before losing to Sugar Ray Leonard in 1981.

Asked if Leonard had hurt him, Hearns said, "Of course he hurt me. I admit it. One thing I never did is underestimate Ray Leonard as a fighter. He's a hell of a man."

Hearns and Leonard sat together at a postfight press conference, exchanging compliments and hoisting each other's arms. Leonard wore dark glasses over his puffy left eye.

"In my book, we are both champions," Leonard said.

Hearns told the Las Vegas crowd, "If you never see another show, you saw one tonight." He also had a message for the fight fans back home. "Detroit," Hearns said, "I shall return."

The end came moments after Leonard caught Hearns flush on the jaw with a looping right, sending Hearns staggering and falling along the ropes.

Leonard, sensing his chance, leaped after Hearns as the Detroiter sagged, stunned on the ropes, and hammered him with heavy blows to the body.

"I definitely knew I was ahead, but there was just one problem. I got hit with a good shot. I thought I was in pretty good control (of my senses), but the ref didn't, and there's nothing I can do."

**THOMAS HEARNS**, on losing on a technical knockout to Sugar Ray Leonard

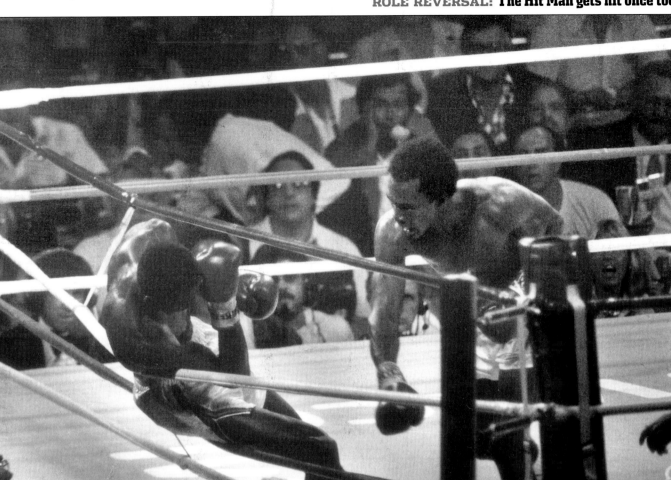

ALAN R. KAMUDA/DETROIT FREE PRESS

Sugar Ray Leonard puts Tommy Hearns on the ropes in their first bout. Their 1989 rematch was a draw. The Free Press' scorecard had Hearns as the winner.

"Of course he hurt me. I admit it. One thing I never did is under-estimate Ray Leonard as a fighter. He's a hell of a man."

**THOMAS HEARNS**, on whether Sugar Ray Leonard hurt him in their first matchup

A stunning left sent Hearns now desperately trying to cover up along the left ropes leading away from his corner.

He was plainly in deep trouble. Referee Davey Pearl leaped forward to signal an end to the fight at 1:45 of the round.

Hearns, the undefeated World Boxing Association welterweight champion entering the bout, said he did not think Pearl should have stopped the fight.

"No, I didn't think the fight should have been stopped," Hearns said. "But those are the breaks. The referee saw different-ly."

"He didn't say anything to me," Pearl said. "He seemed like he knew it was over. He put his head down and headed back to his corner."

Hearns, 22, said Leonard, the 25-year-old World Boxing Council welter-weight champion, hurt him in the sixth round, but he thought he had recovered. He apparently was right, as he began to win rounds on the judges' cards.

But Hearns made an error in the 13th round, and Leonard capitalized on it. Leonard connected with a left hook and then a combi-nation to the head, and it was the beginning of the end

for Hearns. He went down once in the 13th and it was ruled a push, although he seemed helpless draped on the ropes. The second time he went through in almost exactly the same spot. Pearl went to a nine count before Hearns struggled back to the ring.

"I made my mistake by leaving my right hand low and letting Ray counter-punch with good left hooks," said Hearns, whose record dropped to 32-1. "He hit me with some good body shots. My body was in perfect shape, but not my head.

"Of course, I want a rematch. I think I deserve

one."

It was a remarkable per-formance by Leonard, who proved without a doubt that he is the finest crafts-man in the ring today. He had survived his own moments of peril, changed his style, and changed again to wither Hearns.

"I was afraid of the right hand of his until the very end," Leonard said. "He dropped some real bombs on me, and I knew he had another one left.

"I pulled this one out by reaching down in my guts, into my heart. I knew I had to pull out the reserve, and I did."

**40**

THE DATE: April 12, 1942

THE LOCATION: Olympia Stadium, Detroit

THE SETUP:
The shocking 1942 Red Wings jumped to a 3-0 series lead in the Stanley Cup finals, only to lose the last four games — the only team in major sports history to lose a 3-0 lead in a finals. It all unraveled in Game 4, when ...

THE ELEMENTS

# The Wings saw Red

By BERNIE CZARNIECKI

*Editor's note: Reprinted from a 1997 retrospective piece on the Red Wings.*

While World War II raged in Europe and the Pacific, a one-of-a-kind hockey series was played in Detroit and Toronto in 1942.

For the only time in major league sports history, a team lost a 3-0 lead in a best-of-seven finals. The Red Wings were the losers, the Toronto Maple Leafs the winners.

The series was improbable — Wings coach Jack Adams was suspended in the midst of the turnaround — but so was Detroit's entire season.

The fifth-place Red Wings qualified for the playoffs with a 19-25-4 record. Then they unexpectedly beat the Montreal Canadiens and Boston Bruins in the first two rounds — thanks to their famed Liniment Line of Sid Abel, Don Grosso and Eddie Wares and their combined 13 goals.

The finals pitted the Wings against Toronto, the league's No. 2 team.

More surprising, the Wings stunned the Maple Leafs by winning the first three games and appeared poised to sweep.

But Game 4 in Detroit was one for the ages.

After a scoreless first period, the Wings struck first with second-period goals from Mud Bruneteau and Abel.

Bob Davidson and Lorne Carr scored for Toronto to close out the period at 2-2, but the Wings' Carl Liscombe beat goalie Turk Broda at 4:18 of the third with a 35-foot slap shot that put Detroit on top, 3-2.

At that point, referee Mel Harwood took over.

Moments after Liscombe's goal, Harwood whistled off Detroit's Alex Motter on a tripping penalty, which infuriated Adams and his team. They argued long and hard from the bench. Toronto tied the game on

As a coach with the Wings, Jack Adams guided Detroit to three Stanley Cups. A tirade in the 1942 finals might have cost him another.

---

"**Adams became so wound up he forgot how to coach and change lines.**"
**CARL LISCOMBE**, on Red Wings coach Jack Adams' response to a penalty call that gave the Maple Leafs the winning goal in Game 4 of the 1942 Stanley Cup finals

ASSOCIATED PRESS

NHL president Frank Calder presents the Cup to Maple Leafs captain Syl Apps as Connie Smythe, right, home on leave from his Canadian regiment, applauds.

"Argu- ing got us so high that time in the game that things all went to hell after that. We were awfully shook up."

**CARL LISCOMBE**, on the downfall of the Red Wings in Game 4 of the 1942 Stanley Cup finals

a power-play goal by Syl Apps.

"Arguing got us so high that time in the game that things all went to hell after that," said Liscombe. "We were awfully shook up."

With Adams still fuming over the penalty call, Toronto's Nick Metz beat Wings goalie Johnny Mowers with a 10-footer at 12:45 for a 4-3 lead — the eventual game-winner.

After that, Liscombe said, "Adams became so wound up he forgot how to coach and change lines."

The pot boiled over with 69 seconds left. After an offside call halted a Detroit rush, a fan hurled a hot water bag that nearly hit linesman Sammy Babcock.

Wares jokingly handed the bag to Harwood, who in a fury issued a 10-minute misconduct to Wares. Wares refused to leave the ice until he received an explanation for the penalty.

Harwood ordered the puck to be dropped to begin play, then immediately called another penalty on Detroit for too many men on the ice, and ordered Grosso to serve the penalty.

When Grosso overheard Harwood ordering a $50 fine to Wares, he laid his gloves and stick at Harwood's feet and was fined $25.

A record crowd of 13,694 at Olympia Stadium was just as infuriated, littering the ice with debris.

"It was an absolute disgrace the way the referee called so many penalties against us," Liscombe said. Adams "ended up running on the ice after the referee afterwards. He went berserk."

Adams rushed past linesman Donnie MacFayden and began fighting with Harwood. Losing the fight with Adams and Grosso — and surrounded by angry fans — Harwood retreated off the ice with the help of police.

Adams chased Harwood into the officials room before being restrained.

Adams was suspended from the playoffs by league president Frank Calder. With Wings center Ebbie Goodfellow taking over as acting bench coach, the deflated Wings lost the last three games, 9-3, 3-0 and 3-1.

Abel said he couldn't recall much about the incident other than "Adams being really upset."

**THE SETUP:**
The visiting Lions had a 17-16 lead over New Orleans with 11 seconds left. The Saints lined up for a field goal 63 yards away. Their kicker had missed 10 of 15 attempts and only had half a right foot. His attempt would be remembered as ...

**THE ELEMENTS**

# Half a foot, one big boot

## BY JACK SAYLOR

**N**ot all the miracles happen on 34th Street.

One happened here in the gathering gloom at Tulane Stadium with Tom Dempsey, a 23-year-old man who was born with only half a right foot, as the unlikely hero.

Dempsey booted a 63-yard field goal, the longest in pro football history, as time expired to give the New Orleans Saints a 19-17 decision, sending the Lions off the field in a state of shock and 66,910 fans into pandemonium.

Dempsey's thundering kick wiped out a 17-16 Detroit lead, established on Errol Mann's 17-yard field goal with 11 seconds left that seemingly had given the Lions an uphill victory in their bid to stay in Central Division contention.

The dramatics of the final moments transcended all that happened before in a penalty-filled game, frustrating for both Detroit, which couldn't take advantage of most of them, and the Saints, who were recipients of most of them.

But the Saints, who had been sinners most of the game, overcame all to make the coaching debut of J.D. Roberts a smashing success.

Roberts, however, had to play a background role to the pudgy Dempsey, who had hit only five of 15 previous attempts this season.

"They won the game with a miracle," Joe Schmidt said in the stony silence of the Lions' locker room as players showered and dressed slowly in a state of disbelief.

"A miracle," echoed Mike Lucci at the other end of the gloomy dressing room.

"Unbelievable," Mann said.

"It's hard to understand," murmured Wayne Walker, "... a miracle. Bobby Thomson's home run, nothing compares to it."

The stage was set for the fantastic ending after the Saints had finally erased a 14-9 deficit against the stubborn Lions defense as Tom Barrington scored on a three-yard run, giving New Orleans a 16-14 lead.

With fewer than seven minutes remaining, Schmidt had turned to Greg Landry after the Saints had badgered Bill Munson with three interceptions.

Landry drove the team from the Lions' 14 into New Orleans territory as time waned and Mann knelt nervously at the sideline, seeing a game-

---

**"It's hard to understand ... a miracle. Bobby Thomson's home run, nothing compares to it."**

**WAYNE WALKER**, on New Orleans kicker Tom Dempsey's 63-yard field goal to beat the Lions in 1970

"When he hit it, I could tell it was a hell of a impact and I said, 'Oh, my God.' "

**BILL McPEAK**, Lions assistant coach, on New Orleans kicker Tom Dempsey's 63-yard field goal to win the game as time expired

ASSOCIATED PRESS

The Lions gave the Saints only 11 seconds to work with on their final drive. It was enough time for Tom Dempsey to boot a 63-yarder. The Lions would lose the next week, but rally to finish the regular season on a five-game winning streak. Detroit lost, 5-0, in the playoffs to the Dallas Cowboys.

winning field-goal try developing.

With two minutes left, the Lions had a first down at the Saints 35. Mel Farr made five yards and Landry ran for 12. Now 1:15 remained.

Landry tried to maneuver into prime position for Mann. Farr made three and Landry sneaked six to the Saints 9.

Seventeen seconds left. Farr ran at left tackle and time was called with 14 seconds on the clock.

Schmidt declined to run the clock any further and on came Mann.

Mann's kick was true, and with 11 seconds left what could happen?

The Saints ran the kickoff return out of bounds at their 28 with eight seconds left. Bill Kilmer then found Al Dodd with a sideline toss at the 45 with two seconds left.

Holder Joe Scarpati set the snap down behind the New Orleans 38 and Dempsey swung his feet.

"When he hit it, I could tell it was a hell of a impact and I said, 'Oh, my God,' " said Lions assistant Bill McPeak.

The ball soared high and the Lions watched helplessly as incredibly, the ball fell over the crossbar 63 yards away with a little distance to spare.

The previous NFL distance record for field goals, 56 yards, was a kick by Bert Rechichar of the Baltimore Colts against the Chicago Bears on

Sept. 27, 1953. Dempsey had booted a 55-yarder against the Los Angeles Rams a year before his record-breaker.

Dempsey, who was born with a stub of a right hand as well as the deformed foot, doesn't consider himself handicapped. "I've always been able to do anything anybody else did," he said.

As it developed, he can do one thing nobody else can do — kick a 63-yard field goal.

**42**

THE SETUP:
The Michigan State women trailed perennial powerhouse Tennessee by 16 with less than 15 minutes left. But their 'refuse to lose' attitude kept them hustling and hitting shots in a Final Four flurry. In the end, they became the ...

THE
ELEMENTS

# Comeback queens

RASHAUN RUCKER/DETROIT FREE PRESS

### By MICHAEL ROSENBERG

Frame it, seal it, get a videotape of it, enjoy it. Hold on to it forever. Michigan State beat Tennessee, 68-64, but this was so much more than a simple score, so much bigger than a single victory.

It's not just that Tennessee was the favorite in every way — to the experts, and in the hearts of most fans at the RCA Dome. It's not just that Tennessee is the biggest, boldest name in women's college basketball.

No, it's how this happened. Hope and Chance had both checked out of the MSU hotel. With less than 15 minutes left, Tennessee led, 49-33.

Then the Spartans came back and stunned the whole dome. In the final minute of this national semifinal,

"We refuse to lose. Simple. It's been our thing all year. We come back from Notre Dame, (six) points down with like 30 seconds left in the game. We never give up. We just don't."

**VICTORIA LUCAS-PERRY**, above, on MSU's rally from a 16-point deficit against Tennessee in the 2005 NCAA tournament

KIRTHMON F. DOZIER/DETROIT FREE PRESS

The Spartans played it cool in the locker room after beating Tennessee in the national semifinal. But, before they went inside, Liz Shimek, left, and Lindsay Bowen whooped it up.

**COMEBACK QUEENS: MSU vaults past Vols in 2005 Final Four**

> "I would call it 'making plays.' It's pretty powerful when a lot of different people step up."
>
> **JOANNE P. McCALLIE,** Michigan State coach, on her team's comeback

DAVID P. GILKEY/DETROIT FREE PRESS

MSU's Kristin Haynie races for a breakaway lay-up after stealing a pass intended for Tennessee's Loree Moore. Haynie's lay-up gave MSU a 64-62 lead.

Kelli Roehrig scored to give Michigan State a 66-64 lead, and then the Lady Vols had one last desperate chance. And they missed.

And they got the rebound.

And the Vols shot, again and again, but then Roehrig grabbed a rebound and passed to Lindsay Bowen, who found a streaking Victoria Lucas-Perry, who sank a lay-up and the

Lady Vols, all in one flash.

On to the championship game against Baylor.

"We refuse to lose," Lucas-Perry said. "Simple. It's been our thing all year. We come back from Notre Dame, (six) points down with like 30 seconds left in the game. We never give up. We just don't."

Yeah, but when you're down 16 in the second half, don't you start to wonder if ...

"Like I said," Lucas-Perry said, "we don't think we're going to lose."

Fine. But let's be clear: Anybody with a shred of common sense thought otherwise. In the city that hosts the Indy 500, the Spartans led for a few laps and then they spun into a wall, and the sight of it was so ghastly that after a bit, you forgot about winning. You just hoped they walked away safely.

In the middle of the game, Tennessee went on a 32-9 run. Hold on. Can we call that a run? How about a marathon, where one side is sprinting and doing cartwheels, and the other side is wearing lead weights?

During that ... stretch, the Vols totally dominated, which they have done so often in the last two-plus decades that they could patent the phrase. But MSU would not just walk away safely. That was never good enough for these Spartans. They would claw back into the game.

They would win it.

A basket here, a defensive stop there, and the next thing you knew, Bowen was launching a three-pointer from the corner, and when it went in, MSU was within four.

Quick glance up at the clock ... official time

remaining: Way, Way More Than Enough.

The Vols opened another lead. The Spartans kept chipping away. Soon there was Lucas-Perry, this time from the opposite corner, launching another three ... good! MSU was within one. Suddenly, stunningly, there was hope.

Finally, Lucas-Perry sank two free throws to tie the game. Kristin Haynie stole the ball and scored to give MSU a 64-62 lead.

Pretty soon, coach Joanne P. McCallie's Spartans were knee-deep in insanity. Again. Just like against Stanford the previous week. Just like against Southern Cal the week before.

Welcome to the NCAA's newest sport: Supernatural Basketball.

McCallie laughed and said, "Well, I guess it could be called that, but I would call it 'making plays.' It's pretty powerful when a lot of different people step up."

Somebody asked Lucas-Perry how she coolly hit three of four three-pointers. Wasn't her blood flowing at all?

Lucas-Perry laughed and said, "I was open."

In the locker room, the Spartans acted as if they had just beat Eastern Illinois in December. This is all normal to them. For anybody who thought the Spartans would remain outside the women's basketball establishment, Michigan State came within one victory of a national championship, thanks to one of the greatest games the school has ever played, in any sport.

PHOTOS BY RASHAUN RUCKER/DETROIT FREE PRESS

Kristin Haynie, guarding Tennessee's Sidney Spencer, and MSU's defense got tough on the Vols. MSU rallied from a 16-point deficit in the second half, which matched a women's Final Four record. The Spartans' run ended on a sour note in the title game when they lost to Baylor.

For Vols coach Pat Summitt, the dean of women's hoops, losing to MSU was tough to take. "Obviously, this is a very disappointing loss, and it will be a long time until I get this one out of my system."

**NOT TILL THE FAT LADY SINGS 153**

**43**

**THE DATE:** March 22, 1957

**THE LOCATION:** Municipal Auditorium, Kansas City, Mo.

**THE SETUP:**
In the 1957 NCAA basketball semifinals, MSU matched baskets with favored North Carolina. When Jack Quiggle's last-second heave in regulation was ruled too late, North Carolina took three overtimes to prevail, leaving MSU ...

# Out of luck, out of time

By **TOMMY DEVINE**

**M**ighty North Carolina grabbed another of basketball's golden rings when it edged Michigan State, 74-70, in three overtimes in the semifinals of the National Collegiate tournament.

A sellout crowd of 10,500 fans was in an uproar throughout a tight, tense battle that was the second-largest contest played in the 19-year history of this cage classic.

This was a battle that repeatedly hinged on little things; it was a battle in which a split second brought heartbreak to the Spartans and which, by perverse fate, a tick of the timer's clock provided a ledge on which North Carolina managed to hang by its fingertips before it finally pulled out the triumph.

It was North Carolina All-American ace Lennie Rosenbluth who finally broke the Spartans' back with two quick field goals at the outset of the third extra period.

A basket by Carolina's Bob Young and two free throws by Tommy Kearns were trimmings, which offset a field goal by Jack Quiggle and Bob Anderegg's two foul tosses.

Rosenbluth, who scored 846 points during the 30 games of the regular season and then added 91 more in three earlier tournament ballets, turned in another dazzling game.

He dropped in 29 points to take scoring honors. Despite his scoring total, it is doubtful if Rosenbluth ever put in a tougher night.

John Green, Michigan State's superlative sophomore, drew the assignment of guarding Rosenbluth,

holding him to four field goals in the first half.

Over that stretch Rosenbluth had 20 shots, but Green was harassing him constantly so that he seldom could get set or drive for the basket.

In the second half, Green drove the Tar Heel ace from his usual pivot position. Rosenbluth is so talented a shot-maker, however, that it turned into an advantage rather than a handicap.

He hit more consistently from outside than he had when operating from the pivot spot.

With the score tied, 58-58, North Carolina missed a shot with three seconds to go. The Spartans got the rebound and at midcourt Quiggle let loose with a long shot.

The ball swished through the nets as bedlam rocked the giant city audi-

**The ball swished through the nets as bedlam rocked the giant city auditorium. For a fleeting second, everyone thought the Spartans had won with a storybook finish.**

North Carolina coach Frank McGuire, right, breathes a sigh of relief after surviving three overtimes against MSU in the 1957 national semifinal.

To the eternal credit of the Tar Heels, they never allowed the mounting tension to affect them. They were cool and deliberate and finally forced MSU into costly mistakes.

torium. For a fleeting second, everyone thought the Spartans had won with a storybook finish.

But referees Al Lightner and Cliff Ogden ruled the timer's horn had sounded before the ball left Quiggle's hand.

That sent the game into the first overtime.

Then with only 24 seconds of the first extra period remaining, Quiggle slipped under the basket for a lay-up to put the Spartans in front, 64-62.

Fifteen seconds later, Green was fouled and had the chance to put the game beyond the Tar Heels' reach. But Johnny Green missed the shot and North Carolina grabbed the rebound.

With only two seconds to go, the Spartans still held the precious lead. But then Pete Brennan hit from the side and the score was tied, 64-64, and another overtime was on tap.

In the second overtime, Rosenbluth dropped a jump shot from the circle in the opening minute of play. That held up until only 56 seconds remained in the period. Then Green tipped in a shot to tie it

again and bring on the third overtime.

To the eternal credit of the Tar Heels, they never allowed the mounting tension to affect them. They were cool and deliberate and finally forced MSU into costly mistakes.

Rosenbluth's magnificent shooting rightfully was the deciding factor. He first hit from the side. Then after Quiggle tied it, Lennie Rosenbluth dropped another on a jump shot from the circle.

That actually was the finishing touch to the Spartans' gallant bid.

Kearns' two free throws and Young's basket merely provided a cushion.

North Carolina hopped off to a quick 6-0 lead in the opening minute of play. That was the widest margin that ever separated the teams.

The score was tied six times and the lead changed hands nine times during the hectic first half.

In the second half, neither team ever was able to get more than a four-point bulge. And as soon as a lead was established, the rival promptly wiped it out.

**THE DATE:** March 21, 1959

**THE LOCATION:** Jenison Fieldhouse, East Lansing

**THE SETUP:**
Hamtramck was ranked No. 2. Lansing Sexton wasn't expecting much, with no starters taller than 6 feet. The two met in the Class A title game. Hamtramck led by 15 with less than four minutes left, but Sexton ended up with a ...

**THE ELEMENTS**

# Small team, tall title

**BY MICK McCABE**

*Editor's note: Taken from a 1999 retrospective piece*

The game took place 40 years ago, but that makes little difference to Art Frank.

"Hardly a day goes by that I don't think about it," he said.

The comeback was 40 years ago, but don't try telling Clayton Kowalk it was that long ago.

"Anytime I'm in a group of old-timers, that subject always comes up," he said.

The shot was 40 years ago for an 80-79 overtime win, but Bob Davis has yet to figure out why he ended up with the ball in his hands and the final seconds ticking away.

"I still say, 'Why me?' " Davis said.

Yes, it has been 40 years since Hamtramck and Lansing Sexton met for the 1959 Class A state boys basketball championship, and no title game — before or since — has matched it for raw drama.

When the tournament began, Pontiac Central was ranked No. 1 in the state and Hamtramck was a close No. 2.

Lansing Sexton? Please.

The Big Reds had struggled to a 9-7 regular-season record. The lineup featured only two seniors, one of whom graduated in January.

"It was a Cinderella team," said Kowalk, the team's coach.

A very short Cinderella. Sexton did not have a starter 6 feet or taller.

"Our motto was: 'We're short, but don't sell us short,' " recalled Kowalk, who had a knack for coming up with little sayings now and again.

When the tournament began, no one dreamed Sexton was about to make one of the most memorable championship runs in state history.

"To be honest, no, I didn't think we were going to go on and win the state championship," said Chris Ferguson, the team's lone senior in the playoffs. "But I remember during the season Coach told us we were a tournament-type team."

Hamtramck had a tremendous size advantage. The Cosmos featured hulking center John Dobroczynski, 6-5, who was an intimidating inside force. Sexton featured 5-11 Brian Ferguson at center.

Of course, the Sexton players didn't realize they were supposed to lose.

"I never let the kids take the court unless they thought they were going to win," Kowalk said.

---

**"The top of my head was pulsating. The emotions came afterward. I still get goose bumps when I talk about it."**
**CLAYTON KOWALK**, Lansing Sexton coach, on his 9-7 squad's upset win over No. 2 Hamtramck in the 1959 Class A title game

Bob Davis' winning shot, pictured here, bounced twice on the rim before falling through to give Lansing Sexton, dressed in the dark uniforms, an 80-79 victory over Hamtramck in the state's Class A boys basketball title game.

DETROIT FREE PRESS

"I was thinking: 'We've come back so far to lose it on the last shot. Why do I have to be the one to take the shot?' "

**BOB DAVIS**, Lansing Sexton player, on taking the final shot -- and making it -- of the 1959 Class A boys basketball title game

Hamtramck blew the game open with a 26-10 second quarter, taking a commanding 43-26 half-time lead.

"I still figured we had a chance," Kowalk said. "I told the kids: 'We didn't get this far with our chins on our chest and you're not going to leave this locker room that way.' "

Even with 3:52 to play, Hamtramck enjoyed a 72-57 advantage, and the state title appeared to be in the bag.

But then something strange happened. Hamtramck coach Frank Wozniak removed Dobroczynski and captain Art Reid from the game. Dobroczynski hit nine of 16 shots for 22 points and was playing the finest game of his career.

Hamtramck went into a stall, but it couldn't hold onto the ball and Sexton scored the final 15 points of regulation.

"I think our press was starting to work and they were fatigued," Frank said. "Along with the fatigue were some bad decisions."

Sexton then had the ball in the final seconds of overtime, trailing by one, but had no set play and had not determined who would take the final shot.

"We had a team concept," Kowalk said. "We ran our half-court offense and just kept working it until we got a good shot."

With time winding down, Ralph Barnett passed the ball to Davis on the wing, outside the lane.

As he caught the ball, Davis knew time was running out. "I was thinking: 'We've come back so far to lose it on the last shot. Why do I have to be the one to take the shot?' " Davis said.

But he did take the shot because he had no other option. While the ball was in the air, the buzzer sounded.

The ball hit the rim and bounced straight up. It came down and hit the rim and bounced again, then came down through the net.

"There was deafening silence," said Chris Ferguson. "For two seconds nobody said anything. Then there was this explosion of noise with people running on the court."

Kowalk stood on the sideline and watched the celebration in disbelief.

"The top of my head was pulsating," he said. "The emotions came afterwards. I still get goose bumps when I talk about it."

**THE SETUP:**
Gary Player came into the 1972 PGA Championship upset about the Free Press' suggestion that he'd faded. A strong third round put him under par, but he hit the 16th hole of the fourth round still trailing by one. From the rough, he unleashed...

**THE
ELEMENTS**

# A 'monster' shot

BY CURT SYLVESTER AND HOWARD ERICKSON

Years from now, Gary Player is going to come back to Oakland Hills.

Perhaps it will be only in his memory. But, when he does, he's going to stop on the No. 16 hole and recall the shot that won the PGA Championship of 1972 — perhaps the finest shot he has ever made.

Player, a South African who has competed everywhere golf is played, failed to destroy "The Monster" in posting a two-over-par 72 in the final round to go with his previous scores of 71-71-67.

But then, he didn't need to. His one-over-par 281 total after 72 holes was two strokes better than Jim Jamieson and Tommy Aaron, who tied for second at 283.

"The nine-iron at No. 16 has to be one of my greatest shots ever," he mused, just minutes after accepting the championship trophy.

The only shot Player could think of that could compare with it was one he made some years ago on a course in Scotland. For right now, though, this was THE shot of Player's life.

"I couldn't even see the green," he recalled. "I could only see the flag so I had to pick a spot and hit to it. I picked a seat stick (in the gallery) right in front of me.

"I had to gamble; it was either going to be there or in the water in front of the green."

As it turned out, his shot carried across the pond guarding the No. 16 hole and left him with a six-foot birdie putt. He said unhesitatingly that was the hole "that won the tour-nament."

The birdie took the pressure off, although Player said he never considered failure as he approached the final two holes.

"No sir," he declared staunchly. "Because I knew the fellows in front of me were playing those holes, too. When Ben Hogan said this course is a 'monster,' he wasn't mistaken."

The 35-year-old veteran of 17 years on the American circuit pocketed $45,000 in winning the 54th PGA Championship, which rewrote all attendance marks.

An official crowd count of 24,100 for the final round pushed attendance for the three practice days and four tournament rounds to 114,287, almost 38,000 more than the previous record.

A slight drizzle, which turned into a

**I could only see the flag so I had to pick a spot and hit to it.**
**I picked a seat stick (in the gallery) right in front of me."**
        **GARY PLAYER**, on his legendary shot out of the rough on the 16th hole of the final round of the 1972 PGA Championship

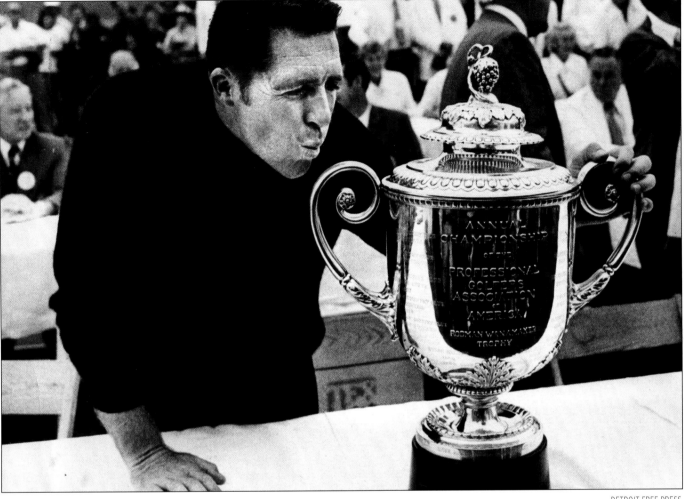

DETROIT FREE PRESS

South African Gary Player took home the PGA Championship trophy and a prize of $45,000 after winning at Oakland Hills in 1972.

"I really felt the pressure at the putt on 18. I don't know if I hurried the putt. I had 1,000 things going through my head."

**JIM JAMIESON**, Kalamazoo native, on finishing his final round with three straight bogeys after leading the field with six holes to go

steady downpour, and a cold wind failed to send the spectators off the course.

By the time Player walked off the 18th green with first prize ensured, they were ringed around the finishing hole in a sea of faces.

Player, the leader at the day's start, went around the 7,054-yard layout conservatively.

Jamieson produced the greatest threat of the day. The chubby pro, who was born in Kalamazoo, gave a wonderful try during the final round, going in front of the field with six holes remaining.

The pressure got too great for him, however. Player regained the lead as Jamieson finished with three straight bogeys.

"I really felt the pressure at the putt on 18," Jamieson said. "I don't know if I hurried the putt. I had 1,000 things going through my head."

But what made the closing holes so tantalizing were some blithering shots by Player himself.

He took bogeys on the 14th and 15th holes, and that put him one behind Jamieson, who already had checked into the clubhouse.

Aaron and Billy Casper also were one behind at

the time and it appeared a playoff wasn't out of the question.

Player extinguished the possibility, though, on No. 16, after slicing his drive off to the left and into the deep rough.

"I was a little despondent at 15 after taking two straight bogeys," he said. "But the gamble came off."

Player said he was given added incentive by two things that occurred during the week. One was a Free Press article that reported that he was not among golf's Big Three anymore.

"That story was unfair," he said. "I've won more

tournaments than anyone else in the game, and I've won more money than anyone except Nicklaus."

He was especially displeased with the headline that accompanied the article, which said he "snorted" at not being included in the Big Three.

"How do you snort anyway?" Player asked.

The other incentive was a telephone call he placed to his father in South Africa.

"My dad is very close to me and he lives for my golf," said Player. "He asked me to win this tournament for him. That gave me added strength."

NOT TILL THE FAT LADY SINGS **159**

**46**

THE SETUP:
The father of Tigers star pitcher Bobo Newsom died after watching his son win Game 1 of the World Series. Newsom dedicated his next start to his dad and won. On one day's rest, Newsom started Game 7. He was sharp, but lost, thanks to ...

THE ELEMENTS

# Bartell's blunder

**By CHARLES P. WARD and JOHN N. SABO**

**D**etroit's fond dreams of a world championship were blasted when Cincinnati's stubborn Reds trounced the Tigers, 2-1, in the seventh and deciding game of the World Series. It was the Reds' first World Series triumph since 1919 when Pat Moran's gallant band trounced Kid Gleason's White Sox in a set of games that later developed into baseball's greatest scandal.

Game 7 was a mound duel between two pitching giants of their respective leagues. Paul Derringer, who was routed by the Tigers in the first game but returned to defeat them in Game 4, was on the mound for the Reds. Louie (Bobo) Newsom was in there for the Tigers.

Newsom, who conquered Derringer in the opening contest and who shut out the Reds with three hits at Detroit in Game 5, was bidding for his third World Series victory. He was bidding for it on only one day's rest.

Bobo Newsom

"We couldn't have expected to get a better pitched game," Tigers manager Del Baker said. "We still lost, and that's that."

Newsom pitched well, as did his victorious opponent; each hurler allowed seven hits. But Newsom had the misfortune of giving up two of the blows in one inning. And he lost because shortstop Richard Bartell, one of the smartest and most alert ballplayers in the Tigers lineup, wasn't as alert as he might have been.

The break of the game came in the seventh inning. Going into the inning, the Tigers were leading, 1-0, and seemed well on their way to victory. Up to that point Newsom yielded only four hits while the Tigers had reached Derringer for six.

But Newsom lost some of the zip on his fastball in the seventh and the Reds began to hit him. Not hard, but just enough. Frank McCormick, the first man up in the inning, doubled to left. Jimmy Ripple then hit a drive to the rightfield screen.

Bruce Campbell faded back slowly, his eyes glued on the ball. When his back came in contact with the screen, he made one frantic leap. The ball eluded his grasp, struck the screen and bounded away for a double. Racing madly after it, Campbell recovered the ball and rifled it

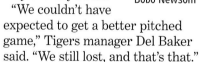

"We couldn't have expected to get a better pitched game. We still lost, and that's that."

**DEL BAKER**, Tigers manager, on Bobo Newsom's attempt to win his third start of the 1940 Series

**"I didn't think there was a play."**

**RICHARD BARTELL**, Tigers shortstop, on his blunder, on which he cut off a throw and failed to notice that the runner heading for home plate hadn't scored yet

The Cincinnati Reds rushed the field to celebrate their Game 7 victory against the Tigers in the 1940 World Series.

toward the infield.

Bartell took the throw and held the ball. He had his back to McCormick and apparently assumed that the Cincinnati first baseman had scored.

But McCormick was only halfway home when Bartell got the ball, and Bartell's teammates shouted excitedly for him to throw to catcher Billy Sullivan. Bartell cocked his arm and turned around. And just then McCormick crossed the plate with the run that tied the score.

It didn't take Cincinnati

skipper Bill McKechnie long to capitalize on the break. He instructed catcher Jimmy Wilson to sacrifice Ripple to third. Ernie Lombardi then batted for Eddie Joost and was given an intentional pass.

Lonnie Frey was sent in to run for Lombardi, who had a sprained ankle. He did not have to run, for Billy Myers hit a fly to Barney McCosky in deep center and Ripple raced home with the run that decided the Series.

"I didn't think there was

a play," Bartell said in the locker room afterward.

Once ahead, Derringer gave the Tigers little chance to stage a comeback. Charlie Gehringer opened the eighth for the Tigers with a solid single to right but was left because Hank Greenberg, Rudy York and Campbell could do nothing to bring him around.

In the ninth, Derringer got rid of Pinky Higgins, Sullivan and Earl Averill, batting for Newsom, with little difficulty. The Series was over.

Derringer, finishing what Bucky Walters started in Game 6 with his 4-0 shutout of the Tigers, enabled the Reds to hold the powerful Bengals to one run in 18 innings.

The Tigers did not seem exceptionally downcast after the game. Their attitude seemed to say, "Well, we shot the works and are satisfied to abide by the result." And, come to think of it, they did very well for a team that was picked by most experts to finish in the second division.

**47**

THE SETUP:

The Red Wings, with the NHL's oldest roster, played the Hurricanes to a 2-all tie in regulation of Game 3 of the 2002 Stanley Cup finals. At 14:47 of the third overtime, the oldest player in the league, 41-year-old center Igor Larionov, scored ...

THE
ELEMENTS

# One for the ages

JULIAN H. GONZALEZ/DETROIT FREE PRESS

Igor Larionov, middle, ended the Game 3 marathon to the delight of teammates Steve Duchesne and Mathieu Dandenault.

BY NICHOLAS J. COTSONIKA

**A**fter 114 minutes and 47 seconds of hockey, after winning a 3-2, triple-overtime thriller, after taking a 2-1 lead over Carolina in the Stanley Cup finals, the Red Wings went to bed.

And stayed awake awhile.

"You're just lying there," forward Kris Draper said. "Your body's asleep, but you're not."

"Your mind is racing," forward Kirk Maltby said. "You're thinking about all the things that happened in the course of the game. It's hard to get to sleep when you're thinking about that kind of stuff. You're telling yourself to sleep, sleep, sleep. But every time you try to stop thinking about it, you just think about it more."

This was a classic. It was the third-longest finals game in history.

Twenty-seven seconds more, and it would have been the longest.

With less than two minutes left in regulation, the Wings trailed, 2-1, and their karma was bad. Captain Steve Yzerman had hit the left post midway through the first period. Defenseman Steve Duchesne had hit the right post early in the third.

Still, they had confidence.

"You have got so many great players and so many guys that can score goals, you never feel like you are out of it," forward

"**You have got so many great players and so many guys that can score goals, you never feel like you are out of it.**"

BRETT HULL, Red Wings forward, on trailing with less than two minutes left in regulation; Hull scored the game-tying goal

"I THINK THIS IS
THE BIGGEST GOAL
OF MY CAREER."

IGOR LARIONOV, on his first playoff overtime goal, which came against Carolina's Arturs Irbe

MANDI WRIGHT/DETROIT FREE PRESS

"Every-body was feeling it a little bit. It was basically one burst of energy and head right to the bench."

**STEVE YZERMAN,** on the Wings' approach to keeping up their energy once Game 2 of the 2002 Stanley Cup finals went into a third overtime

JULIAN H. GONZALEZ/DETROIT FREE PRESS

Wings goalie Dominik Hasek turns Sami Kapanen's bid for glory aside in the second overtime. Hasek faced 22 shots in the overtimes.

Brett Hull said.

Yzerman won a draw in the right circle. Center Sergei Fedorov passed from the right point to the left. Defenseman Nicklas Lidstrom took a shot, and Hull, holding out his stick in the slot, tipped the puck past goal-tender Arturs Irbe.

One minute, 14 seconds remained.

Hull said the play might have been "dumb luck," but Brendan Shanahan said Hull had such awesome hand-eye coordination that it was "not an accident he got his stick on it."

Regardless, the game was tied.

Overtime I.

The chances kept coming. At about 8:35, rookie center Pavel Datsyuk made Gretzky-like moves — stick-handling past forward Sami Kapanen, then defenseman Marek Malik — but Irbe got his left pad on the puck. At about 12:44, one-timing a pass from Fedorov on a 2-on-1, Shanahan fired inches wide left of a yawning net.

At about 15:35, defenseman Fredrik Olausson hit the crossbar.

"You start to wonder if it's ever going to go in," Olausson said.

Overtime II.

The Hurricanes killed a penalty. Then the Wings killed one, although goaltender Dominik Hasek made things interesting by wandering from his net and falling.

Yzerman had the best scoring chance at about 16:39. At the end of a pretty passing play, Shanahan sent the puck from the right wing across the slot.

Yzerman put it on net, but Irbe dove and snagged it with his glove. Yzerman rolled head over heels, then appeared to swear and say, "I don't believe it!"

Said Shanahan: "I was thinking, 'Well, at least I'm not the only guy.' "

Overtime III.

In the Carolina dressing room, players were taking fluid intravenously. In the Detroit dressing room, things were relatively routine.

"I have always thought that youth and enthusiasm will take you only so far," Hull said.

Carolina forward Jaroslav Svoboda

## INSIDE THE FINISH
# What made the end so exciting:

**1** **BY THE NUMBERS**
Crunching the Red Wings-Hurricanes triple-over-time game:

**8:14 P.M.:** Opening face-off.

**11:14:** Time left in regulation when Brett Hull tied the score at 2 and forced overtime.

**1:15 A.M.:** Igor Larionov scored in the third overtime for a 3-2 victory five hours and one minute after the game started.

**114:47:** Actual playing time.

**176:30:** The longest game in playoff history was the Red Wings' 1-0 victory over the Montreal Maroons in the 1936 semifinals. Mud Bruneteau scored in the sixth overtime at 176:30.

**1:** Player who was on the ice the entire time — 'Canes goalie Arturs Irbe. Dominik Hasek was off 25 seconds on delayed penalties.

**52:03:** Ice time logged by Nicklas Lidstrom, the iron man among skaters (Carolina's Bret Hedican was second with 49:34 and Chris Chelios third with 46:38).

**9:28:** Least ice time of any player, the Hurricanes' Kevyn Adams. Pavel Datsyuk was the Wings' low man with 19:48.

**96:** Shots taken in the game — 53 by the Wings, 43 by the Hurricanes.

**.948:** Combined save percentage by Hasek (.953) and Irbe (.943).

**46:** Shots taken in overtime — 24 by the Wings, 22 by the 'Canes.

**.978:** Combined save percentage in overtime by Hasek (1.000) and Irbe (.958).

**3:** Shots taken in the game by Larionov.

**2:** Goals scored by Larionov.

MANDI WRIGHT/DETROIT FREE PRESS

Brett Hull forced overtime when he scored with 1:14 remaining in regulation. En route to the Stanley Cup, Hull scored 10 playoff goals in 2002.

had a chance early in the third overtime.

"I was kind of holding my breath a little bit there," Yzerman said.

As the period went on, both teams were trying to catch their breath.

"Everybody was feeling it a little bit," Yzerman said. "It was basically one burst of energy and head right to the bench."

And what do you know? In the end, the NHL's oldest player had the jump in his legs to end it.

Igor Larionov, the Wings' 41-year-old center, took a pass from forward Tomas Holmstrom on the rush. He stick-handled past diving defender Bates Battaglia.

Then, with defenseman Mathieu Dandenault in front, he backhanded the puck over Irbe and into the roof of the net at 14:47.

"I think this is the biggest goal of my career," said Larionov, who never had scored a playoff overtime goal and became the oldest player ever to score in the finals. "It's obviously huge for me."

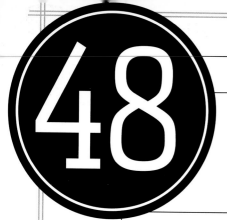

**THE DATE:** February 16, 1977

**THE LOCATION:** Milwaukee Arena, Milwaukee

**THE SETUP:**
Coach Dick Vitale had led Detroit to a 20-game winning streak heading into a game against Al McGuire's Marquette Warriors. In the final seconds, Dennis Boyd hit a jumper and Detroit pulled off a stunner. The city was abuzz after ...

# Dickie V's Titanic upset

**By CHARLIE VINCENT AND CURT SYLVESTER**

No more shrugging off the University of Detroit as just a nice group of men who can't win the big ones.

Dennis Boyd's jump shot from the top of the key as time ran out vaulted the Titans back into the big game and draped an eerie cloak of silence over 10,938 Milwaukee fans, who could hardly believe U-D had upset Marquette, 64-63.

It was fitting that it was Boyd, the Titans' senior captain, who got the one that preserved U-D's 21-game winning streak.

Boyd had almost single-handedly kept the Titans in the game during the first 20 minutes as high-scoring Terry Tyler and John Long contributed just four first-half points.

Thanks to Boyd and Terry Duerod, though, U-D trailed only 32-26 at intermission.

Marquette led through most of the game and at times seemed on the verge of wrapping it up and sending U-D back home, once again relegated to being something less than a first-rate power.

Midway through the first half, the Warriors built a 20-10 lead. But the Titans nibbled away at that to go into halftime with just that six-point deficit.

The second half was just the kind of war Dick Vitale and Marquette coach Al McGuire had warned it would be.

U-D scored the first six points on field goals by Boyd, Tyler and Long and it was all even at 32-all. From there on, it was a clawing, gouging, sweat-and-blood-stained, no-holds-barred riot that saw both teams play some brilliant basketball — and both

played some basketball that made both coaches pale and throw their hands to their faces.

During one stretch, Marquette turned the ball over five times in six possessions.

After making just one of eight field goal attempts in the first half, Long pumped home seven of nine after intermission to lead U-D scorers with 20 points.

Tyler, though, was another matter.

Marquette's Bo Ellis and Jerome Whitehead covered him like a blanket, denying him the ball and intimidating him into errors when he did get it. Tyler finished with just four points and made only two of seven field-goal attempts, but led both teams with nine rebounds and blocked a pair of Ellis' shots.

Ellis finished as Marquette's leading scorer, nevertheless, with 21 points.

**It was fitting that it was Boyd, the Titans' senior captain, who got the one that preserved U-D's 21-game winning streak.**

## INSIDE THE FINISH
# What made the end so exciting:

**MARCH 11, 1999**
**TITANS UPSET UCLA**

INDIANAPOLIS — Ghosts can't beat you, so why fear them?

That's a message Perry Watson embedded in his players' heads every day leading up to Detroit Mercy's NCAA tournament debut against the game's greatest legacy.

As far as Watson could recall, none of the names on the back of those UCLA jerseys resembled the likes of Walton, Wilkes or Wicks.

And the Titans believed as they walked off the floor at halftime, trailing only by two, nodding their heads as if convincing themselves: "Yes, we can play with these guys!"

And they can beat these guys, too. Why ask why?

Just go crazy, Detroit, and celebrate one of the sweetest NCAA tournament moments we've ever enjoyed as the Titans stunned the fabled Bruins, 56-53, in a game they had seemingly let slide through their grasp on many occasions.

"Beat L.A., baby, beat L.A.!" shouted senior Bacari Alexander. "Just like the Pistons against the Lakers. Beat L.A."

Daniel Whye's clutch jumper just before the 35-second shot clock expired kept the Titans ahead for keeps in the closing seconds, and provided another reminder why everyone loves the NCAA tournament. It's one of the few settings on the athletic landscape where heart, determination and indomitable will can overcome talent.

KIRTHMON F. DOZIER/DETROIT FREE PRESS

Detroit's Jermaine Jackson, driving against UCLA's Jaron Rush, led the Titans with 17 points. It was the second straight season Detroit won in the first round of the NCAA tournament. The other victory was against St. John's.

The game reflected what had been a nerve-racking day for everyone at Detroit Mercy. Athletic director Brad Kinsman couldn't eat, sleep or diminish the magnitude of the evening for the university. He acknowledged that a victory over UCLA would be the biggest triumph in the 94-year history of Titans basketball.

"No. 12 seeds have beaten fifth seeds fairly regularly," Kinsman said, "but you're talking about probably the single most distinguishable program of all time in college basketball. You try not to think about it, but you are taking on a legend as well as a team."

In victory, it's easy to see how Detroit Mercy could look at the Bruins and their ilk with more than a touch of envy. Watson would love to get just one of those All-Americas that the UCLAs, Dukes and North Carolinas of the basketball world's upper crust keep moving in and out as if their programs have big revolving doors.

But he and his players reminded us that on this stage, the size of the heart is as critical as the size of the talent or the size of the name.

**By Drew Sharp**

But it was a crucial turnover by Ellis — with just 36 seconds remaining — that supplied the Titans with the chance they needed.

Marquette led, 63-58, with three minutes to go, but after Jeff Whitlow and Boyd scored back-to-back baskets to narrow the margin to one, the Warriors went into a stall.

The delay tactic worked for a minute and a half, then Ellis lost control of a pass in the lane. The ball rolled down his leg and Tyler snatched it away from him.

Detroit deliberately dribbled away all but two of the remaining seconds. Then Boyd, who missed just three of the 10 field goals he attempted, arched the ball cleanly through the hoop and the Titans started celebrating while the fans in the jam-packed arena looked at each other in disbelieving silence.

In Detroit, a roar erupted from the Pistons' locker room and Kevin Porter burst happily out the door.

"They did it," he cried as he pulled his coat up over his shoulder and headed into the cold night.

The University of Detroit had just knocked off Marquette on television in the Detroit dressing room, and the Titans gave the Pistons a bigger thrill than they had given themselves by disposing of the Trail Blazers.

# 49

**THE SETUP:**

The U-M football team did more than just win a game.
The Wolverines did more than just beat previously undefeated Penn State.
With a last-second touchdown, the players proved to be ...

**THE ELEMENTS**

# Resilient to the very end

### By MARK SNYDER

KIRTHMON F. DOZIER/DETROIT FREE PRESS

**N**o one knew what to do. Steve Breaston scaled Michigan Stadium's brick wall twice, each time diving into the crowd with an ear-to-ear grin.

Tim Massaquoi wandered the field, stunned that his dream of beating his home-state team had come true.

And Mario Manningham rode his teammates' shoulders as few Michigan freshmen ever have.

But Michigan linebacker Chris Graham said it best as he bounced around the field.

"We're back!" Graham screamed.

One second from a season-crushing loss, the Michigan football team showed it still has life, stunning No. 8 Penn State, 27-25, in Ann Arbor on a 10-yard touchdown pass from Chad Henne to Manningham with no time left.

The winning play began with one second remaining, but Henne never flinched, even smiling on the drive that set it up, before hitting Manningham with an end-zone strike to cap an improbable 42-second, 53-yard march.

"I just caught it," Manningham said, racing from the field after his teammates lowered him. "We just executed, and I knew someone would come up with it."

Manningham was Henne's second target on the play, but few were surprised he caught the game-winner. After all, he has been Michigan's dramatic playmaker all season, including his spectacular grab to pull the Wolverines from their first deficit, tying the game at 18 more than nine

**"Mario played his butt off, the way he came through. He was injured, he caught the ball, he's a playmaker."**
**STEVE BREASTON**, above, Michigan wide receiver, on teammate Mario Manningham, who caught the winning TD as time expired

"I JUST CAUGHT IT. WE JUST EXECUTED, AND I KNEW SOMEONE WOULD COME UP WITH IT."

**MARIO MANNINGHAM,** on his game-winning touchdown catch as time expired

KIRTHMON F. DOZIER/DETROIT FREE PRESS

"I think Coach Carr must have called (Miss) Cleo or something. He said in the locker room at halftime that it was going to come down to the final play and it did ..."

**GABE WATSON,** Michigan defensive tackle, on coach Lloyd Carr's halftime speech

KIRTHMON F. DOZIER/DETROIT FREE PRESS

U-M's Leon Hall returns an interception from Penn State's Michael Robinson (12) with 3:14 left in the game.

minutes earlier.

"Mario played his butt off," Breaston said. "The way he came through. He was injured, he caught the ball, he's a playmaker."

Pushing through his undisclosed injury, Manningham just did what the Wolverines practiced all week.

While the Wolverines normally spend just Thursday's practice on their late-game offense, the routine changed the week before the Penn State game with three days of the pressure drills.

The catch ended a furious fourth quarter, when the lead changed hands four times and 39 points were scored.

Every time the Wolverines seemed crushed, they found a little more life.

Leading, 10-3, entering the third quarter, Michigan appeared to be in control. But apparently someone pushed the fast-forward button. In a 17-second span opening the fourth quarter, Michigan's world flipped.

Penn State quarterback Michael Robinson ran in a four-yard touchdown to tie the game at 10. On Michigan's next play, Henne was stripped of the ball and watched cornerback Alan Zemaitis return it 35 yards for a touchdown.

Suddenly Michigan was reeling, unsure of how many more chances remained and stunned a third time when a fumbled snap turned into Penn State's two-point conversion.

But Manningham provided the first CPR, reviving Michigan on the next series by streaking down the left sideline to catch Henne's 33-yard touchdown pass.

The beautiful basket grab brought Michigan within two, setting up Mike Hart's two-

KIRTHMON F. DOZIER/DETROIT FREE PRESS

Although this 33-yard TD catch from U-M's Mario Manningham was impressive, it didn't top his second touchdown, a 10-yarder that came with no time left in the fourth quarter.

point run to tie the game.

Michigan regained the lead on a field goal with 3:45 left and again seemed safe.

But that was before Robinson converted a crucial fourth down, then ran for his second touchdown with 53 seconds remaining, pushing the Nittany Lions to an apparent 25-21 victory.

Breaston returned the kickoff 41 yards to the Michigan 47-

yard line on what U-M coach Lloyd Carr called "the biggest play of the game."

All Henne had to do was march his team into the end zone amid a roaring crowd and into the teeth of the Big Ten's second-rated defense. As the Pennsylvania native said, proud of the win, "I can go back home."

Carr's 99th Michigan win mir-

rored his first in 1995, also won on a last-second touchdown catch, over Virginia, also at Michigan Stadium.

"I have had a number of wild games in the past few years, but I have never had a wilder game than this one," Carr said.

It also helps having a prophet on your side, as Carr recovered a crucial two extra seconds for U-M on the last drive, realizing

the clock ran too long when Michigan called a time-out with 30 seconds left.

"I think Coach Carr must have called (Miss) Cleo or something," defensive tackle Gabe Watson said. "He said in the locker room at halftime that it was going to come down to the final play and it did, and we pulled out the victory."

**50**

**THE DATE:** September 2, 1991

**THE LOCATION:** Stadium Court, New York

**THE SETUP:**
Grosse Pointe Woods' Aaron Krickstein was in position to defeat tennis legend Jimmy Connors and advance to the quarterfinals of the U.S. Open. But Connors pulled off an improbable comeback. Krickstein couldn't ruin Connors' ...

# Birthday bonanza

### By GREG STODA

**D**on't blow out the candles. Don't take down the balloons.

This is a Jimmy Connors birthday party that isn't quite ready to end.

Aaron Krickstein couldn't steal the cake.

Connors bullied and limped and screamed and — oh, please, don't forget this verb — willed — his way to a remarkable victory on Stadium Court at the U.S. Open.

What a glorious 39th birthday celebration Connors threw for himself.

Connors twice came from a set down — and from three games behind in the last one — to beat Krickstein, 3-6, 7-6 (10-8), 1-6, 6-3, 7-6 (7-4), and reach the Open quarters.

"This," Connors said, "is what I live for."

Aaron Krickstein

Connors, who has not lost to Krickstein in six career meetings, was constantly on the attack. Krickstein, the maybe too-polite 24-year-old from Grosse Pointe Woods, tried to fight him off for more than 4 1/2 hours.

"I should have been more aggressive," Krickstein said. "I played too deep. He lulls me into that kind of game."

This kind of game: Connors came to the net 137 times to Krickstein's 20 (on 374 points played).

This kind of game: Connors played feast-or-famine with 192 points taken or given away on outright winners or unforced errors.

This kind of game: Connors had 24 break points against Krickstein, but he converted only five.

The last one saved him.

Connors held to get to 3-5 in the fifth set and then — with Krickstein serving for the match — broke him. He first charged the net for a forehand winner at deuce, then scooped a backhand from below the cord to get the game.

They held serve to the tiebreaker, which Connors led almost from the outset. The official winner came when Connors — anticipating Krickstein's shot down the line — placed a backhand block-volley into the open court.

Perfect scene.

Connors at the net. Krickstein at the baseline.

"Yeah, I should have hit the ball

> **"It bothered me. But that's not an excuse. I was up with a chance to win and didn't make the shots."**
>
> **AARON KRICKSTEIN**, on a blister that developed on his right hand during the fifth set

The 15th point of the tiebreaker went to Krickstein, when chair umpire David Littlefield overruled a linesperson's sideline call on the opposite side of the court.

"He called the ball out!" Connors hollered. "You didn't see it. You (bleep). Get your (bleep) out of the chair.

"I'm out here playing my butt off at 39 years old and you're pulling that crap?"

Littlefield's reserved response was that the ball was clearly out.

"Clearly out, my butt," Connors said.

Connors, properly motivated and with his fourth packed Stadium Court crowd in four rounds cheering his every breath, won the next three points, and the sets were square.

Connors took time off in the third set — he won the first game and nothing else.

"I knew he was just trying to get his second wind," Krickstein said.

Maybe the rest helped. Connors got the only break in the fourth set (sixth game), and that set up the remarkable finish.

Krickstein broke to get to 4-2 in the fifth set, but noticed a blister developing at the base of the ring finger on his right serving hand.

"It bothered me," Krickstein said. "But that's not an excuse. I was up with a chance to win and didn't make the shots."

In fact, Krickstein held service in a monstrous eight-deuce seventh game.

Then came Connors' rush.

A blister, and Krickstein dropped the cake.

> "I should have been more aggressive. I played too deep. He lulls me into that kind of game."
>
> **AARON KRICKSTEIN**, on whether his lack of aggressiveness led to a loss in a 4 1/2-hour match in the 1991 U.S. Open

ASSOCIATED PRESS

Jimmy Connors took advantage of Aaron Krickstein's passivity to advance to the quarterfinals of the 1991 U.S. Open.

harder," said Krickstein, who lost a five-set match for only the sixth time in 27 such circumstances. Krickstein did that early and won the first set.

Connors raced to a 5-1 lead in the second set, but Krickstein twice broke his serve to get even. It eventually went to a tiebreaker.

And that was a circus.

Connors led, 1-0.

Krickstein led, 3-1.

Connors led, 5-4.

Krickstein jumped to a set point, 6-5. Connors belted a service winner.

Connors jumped to a set point of his own at 7-6. Krickstein caught him with a cross-court pass.

Circus? Send in the clowns.

# CREDITS

**EDITOR:**
Al Toby

**PHOTO EDITOR:**
Diane Weiss

**COORDINATOR:**
Dave Robinson

**DESIGNER:**
Ryan Ford

**PHOTO SUPPORT:**
Rose Ann McKean

**RESEARCH CHIEF:**
Kelly Solon

**CONTRIBUTING RESEARCHERS:** Kevin Bull, Bill Collison, Bernie Czarniecki, David Darby, Tim Marcinkoski, Mick McCabe, Dave Robinson, Michael Rosenberg, Drew Sharp, Gene Myers

**COVER DESIGN:** Ryan Ford

**TECHNICAL SUPPORT:** A.J. Hartley, Ann Mieczkowski, Stephen Mounteer

**COPY EDITORS:** Kevin Bull, Bill Collison, David Darby, Bob Ellis, Vince Ellis, Marisela de la Garza, Janet Graham, Tim Marcinkoski, Kelly Solon

**SPECIAL THANKS:** Steve Dorsey, Tom Panzenhagen, Gene Myers, Curt Sylvester, Patrice Williams

**VERY SPECIAL THANKS:** Mekeisha Madden Toby, the good folks at Nemo's and The Anchor Bar, the makers of Mountain Dew, and the guy who thought up putting jalapeno peppers on pizza

**FREE PRESS CONTRIBUTING WRITERS:** Jo-Ann Barnas, Jack Berry, Clifton Brown, George Cantor, Nicholas J. Cotsonika, Bernie Czarniecki, Marshall Dann, Tommy Devine, Mike Downey, W.W. Edgar, John Eligon, Howard Erickson, Tommy George, Gene Guidi, Jemele Hill, Johnette Howard, Steve Kornacki, Bob Latshaw, Mick McCabe, Hal McCoy, Corky Meinecke, George Puscas, John N. Sabo, Jack Saylor, George Sipple, Lyall Smith, Mark Snyder, Greg Stoda, Curt Sylvester, Charlie Vincent, Charles P. Ward and Shawn Windsor

**FREE PRESS CONTRIBUTING PHOTOGRAPHERS:** Regina H. Boone, Kirthmon F. Dozier, David P. Gilkey, Julian H. Gonzalez, Hugh Grannum, Alan R. Kamuda, Pauline Lubens, Steven R. Nickerson, Craig Porter, Rashaun Rucker, Eric Seals, Mary Schroeder, Tony Spina, Gabriel B. Tait, Mandi Wright

### COVER PHOTO CREDITS

Front main photo of **Kirk Gibson** by Mary Schroeder/DFP
Front photo of **Ted Lindsay** by Associated Press
Front photo of **Michigan State women's basketball** by Kirthmon F. Dozier/DFP
Front photo of **Joe Louis** from Detroit Free Press files

Front photo of **Rasheed Wallace** by Kirthmon F. Dozier
Front photo of **Igor Larionov** by Mandi Wright/DFP
Front photo of the **1953 NFL championship game** from Detroit Lions
Front photo of **Charles Woodson** by Julian H. Gonzalez/DFP

Back photo of **Steve Yzerman** by Detroit Free Press
Back photo of **Chris Webber** by Susan Ragan/AP
Back photo of **Rumeal Robinson** by Steven R. Nickerson/DFP